RETIREMENT ISSUES, PLANS AND LIFESTYLES

PRIVATE-SECTOR PENSIONS

ASSESSMENTS OF DISCLOSURE AND REPORTING REQUIREMENTS

RETIREMENT ISSUES, PLANS AND LIFESTYLES

Additional books in this series can be found on Nova's website under the Series tab.

Additional e-books in this series can be found on Nova's website under the e-book tab.

RETIREMENT ISSUES, PLANS AND LIFESTYLES

PRIVATE-SECTOR PENSIONS

ASSESSMENTS OF DISCLOSURE AND REPORTING REQUIREMENTS

CHRISTIAN WONG
EDITOR

nova publishers
New York

NOTICE TO THE READER

Library of Congress Cataloging-in-Publication Data

ISBN: 978-1-63482-608-2

Published by Nova Science Publishers, Inc. † New York

CONTENTS

PREFACE

This book examines the reports and disclosures pension plans are required to make to government agencies and plan participants; the ways, if any, reports to agencies may be inefficient or ineffective; and the ways, if any, disclosures to participants may be inefficient or ineffective. The book also discusses the extent to which law and regulations permit electronic disclosure to participants; explores the reported advantages and disadvantages associated with electronic delivery; and evaluates the weaknesses identified, if any, in the agencies' electronic delivery requirements.

Chapter 1 – The private sector pension system in the United States represents trillions of dollars in assets and is a key source of financial security for millions of Americans. To promote transparency and enhance retirement security, legislation and regulations require that plan sponsors provide numerous reports to Labor, IRS, and PBGC, and numerous disclosures to plan participants. GAO was asked to review this system of private sector pension plan reporting and disclosure.

In this report, GAO examined (1) the reports and disclosures pension plans are required to make to government agencies and plan participants; (2) the ways, if any, reports to agencies may be inefficient or ineffective, and (3) the ways, if any, disclosures to participants may be inefficient or ineffective. In conducting this work, GAO reviewed relevant statutes and regulations; analyzed inquiries to Labor's participant help line; assessed certain disclosures for readability when evaluated against criteria based on federal plain language guidelines; and interviewed agency officials, plan sponsor representatives, service providers, and participant advocates.

Chapter 2 – With the advent of new technology, sponsors of U.S. private-sector pension plans have begun to deliver plan information to participants electronically in an effort to reduce plan costs and provide greater participant choice. Yet there are concerns that use of electronic disclosure could make it more difficult for some plan participants to receive important information about their plans. GAO was asked to review issues related to electronic disclosure. For this report, GAO: (1) examined the extent to which law and regulations permit electronic disclosure to participants; (2) explored the reported advantages and disadvantages associated with electronic delivery; and (3) evaluated the weaknesses identified, if any, in the agencies' electronic delivery requirements. In conducting this work, GAO reviewed and analyzed relevant federal statutes and regulations; stakeholder responses to Labor's 2011 request for information on electronic disclosure; and any weaknesses identified in interviews of participant advocates and industry representatives, selected by GAO to capture a broad array of perspectives.

In: Private-Sector Pensions
Editor: Christian Wong

ISBN: 978-1-63482-608-2

Chapter 1

PRIVATE PENSIONS: CLARITY OF REQUIRED REPORTS AND DISCLOSURES COULD BE IMPROVED*

United States Government Accountability Office

WHY GAO DID THIS STUDY

The private sector pension system in the United States represents trillions of dollars in assets and is a key source of financial security for millions of Americans. To promote transparency and enhance retirement security, legislation and regulations require that plan sponsors provide numerous reports to Labor, IRS, and PBGC, and numerous disclosures to plan participants. GAO was asked to review this system of private sector pension plan reporting and disclosure.

In this report, GAO examined (1) the reports and disclosures pension plans are required to make to government agencies and plan participants; (2) the ways, if any, reports to agencies may be inefficient or ineffective, and (3) the ways, if any, disclosures to participants may be inefficient or ineffective. In conducting this work, GAO reviewed relevant statutes and regulations; analyzed inquiries to Labor's participant help line; assessed certain disclosures for readability when evaluated against criteria based on federal plain language

* This is an edited, reformatted and augmented version of a United States Government Accountability Office publication, No. GAO-14-92, dated November 2013.

guidelines; and interviewed agency officials, plan sponsor representatives, service providers, and participant advocates.

What GAO Recommends

GAO asks Congress to consider shifting responsibility and necessary resources to Labor for managing the pension benefit data that SSA provides to retirees. GAO also recommends that the agencies improve their online tools on reporting requirements and facilitate better readability of disclosures. In response, the agencies generally agreed with our findings and are taking steps to address the issues we identified.

What GAO Found

Sponsors of private sector pension plans are required to submit various reports to federal agencies and disclosures to participants depending on the plans' type, size, and circumstances. GAO identified more than 130 reports and disclosures stemming from provisions of the Employee Retirement Income Security Act of 1974, as amended (ERISA), and the Internal Revenue Code, as administered largely by three ERISA agencies: the Department of Labor (Labor), Internal Revenue Service (IRS), and Pension Benefit Guaranty Corporation (PBGC). Although each plan sponsor is required to submit only certain of these reports and disclosures, determining which ones can be challenging and the agencies' online resources to aid plan sponsors with this task are neither comprehensive nor up-to-date.

Plan sponsors' reports to the ERISA agencies involve minimal duplication, but the management of data on one report raised concerns. Notices that the Social Security Administration (SSA) sends to retirees listing vested benefits left behind with previous employers can be misleading, because management of the data is fragmented across three agencies and none assumes responsibility for ensuring the data are accurate. Beyond issuing the form and instructions, IRS views its role as merely to pass the data through from sponsors to SSA, SSA views its role as merely to provide retirees with whatever data SSA receives from IRS, and Labor views its role as merely to respond to retirees' inquiries. As a result, the SSA notices can be misleading, listing benefits that have already been paid.

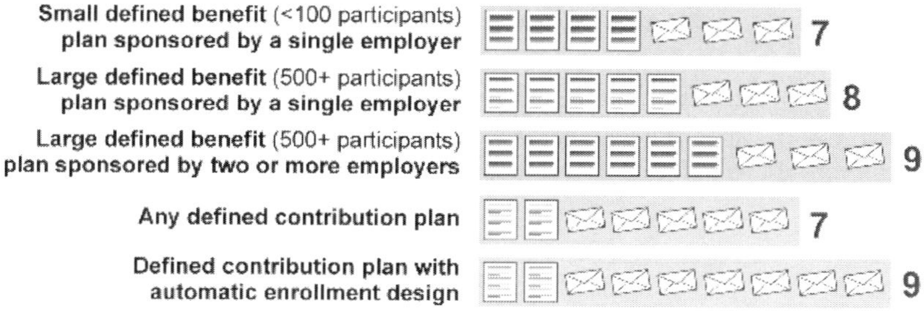

Source: GAO analysis of statute and agency information.

Note: Most routine reports and disclosures are required annually. Additional routine and nonroutine reports and disclosures may be required depending on a plan's design and circumstances.

Number of Routine Reports and Disclosures Required under ERISA Varies Based on Plan Characteristics.

Participant disclosures are numerous and do not always communicate effectively. Various groups GAO interviewed said that participants often find the content overwhelming and confusing. Although certain disclosures are required by law to be written in a manner calculated to be understood by the average plan participant, the three ERISA agencies acknowledged that enforcement of these provisions has not been a priority. Also, GAO found that several model notices that these agencies had developed as templates for sponsors to use in developing their disclosures fell short when evaluated against federal plain language guidelines.

ABBREVIATIONS

DB	defined benefit
DC	defined contribution
EAC	ERISA Advisory Council
EACA	eligible automatic contribution arrangement
ERISA	Employee Retirement Income Security Act of 1974
FKGL	Flesch-Kincaid Grade-Level
FTAP	funding target attainment percentage
IRA	individual retirement account
IRC	Internal Revenue Code
IRS	Internal Revenue Service

OMB	Office of Management and Budget
PBGC	Pension Benefit Guaranty Corporation
PPA	Pension Protection Act of 2006
QACA	qualified automatic contribution arrangements
QDIA	qualified default investment alternatives
SEC	Securities and Exchange Commission
SPD	summary plan description
SSA	Social Security Administration

* * *

November 21, 2013

Congressional Requesters

The private sector pension system in the United States represents trillions of dollars in assets and is a key source of financial security for nearly 130 million Americans. The framework of reports and disclosures is intended to ensure that plans are operated in accordance with certain prescribed standards and that sufficient information is provided to protect participant rights and help participants make informed retirement planning decisions. Congress has attempted to promote transparency and enhance retirement security by incorporating reporting and disclosure requirements into legislation. The Employee Retirement Income Security Act of 1974 (ERISA),[1] requires private sector pension plan sponsors, fiduciaries, administrators, or other third parties[2] to report certain information to federal agencies, including the Department of Labor (Labor), the Pension Benefit Guaranty Corporation (PBGC), and the Department of the Treasury's (Treasury) Internal Revenue Service (IRS). ERISA also requires plan sponsors to provide information, generally referred to as disclosures, to plan participants.[3]

Recognizing that the system of pension plan reports and disclosures has become more complex over time, you requested that we look at how useful all the pension reporting and disclosure requirements are to sponsors, participants, and government officials and determine whether there are ways to improve the system. This report 1) describes the reports and disclosures that sponsors of private sector pension plans may be required to provide to government agencies and plan participants; 2) identifies the ways, if any, that required reports to agencies may be inefficient or ineffective; and 3) identifies the ways, if any, that required disclosures to participants may be inefficient or ineffective.

To determine what reports and disclosures pension plan sponsors are required to provide to federal agencies and plan participants, respectively, we compiled available lists and other information about reports and disclosures from agency websites and lists from three service provider websites. The assembled information included details about who must submit information; to whom it must be provided; citations to federal laws, regulations, guidance, forms, and model notices;[4] and events and circumstances that trigger reports and disclosures. We then worked with officials at the agencies—Labor, IRS, and PBGC—to revise and update the list and add details about agency reports and participant disclosures. We also reviewed relevant federal laws and regulations to verify selected information.

To identify the ways reports and disclosures may be inefficient or ineffective, we interviewed representatives from nine associations, two plan sponsors, six service providers, and four participant advocacy groups, and reviewed data on 1 year of participant calls to Labor's call center for benefit assistance.[5] The interview information cannot be generalized beyond the individuals we interviewed, but we selected the groups to represent a wide range of differing perspectives on any issues with and ways to improve the preparation and use of the information provided. We also interviewed officials at PBGC, IRS, and Labor to obtain their perspective on the efficiency and effectiveness of the reporting and disclosure process. In addition, we evaluated selected reports to agencies for redundancy, and we evaluated the readability of certain model notices produced by Labor and IRS to help plan sponsors prepare required disclosures. (For a more detailed description of our readability analysis, see app. I.)

We conducted this performance audit from July 2012 through October 2013 in accordance with generally accepted government auditing standards. Those standards require that we plan and perform the audit to obtain sufficient, appropriate evidence to provide a reasonable basis for our findings and conclusions based on our audit objectives. We believe that the evidence obtained provides a reasonable basis for our findings and conclusions based on our audit objectives.

BACKGROUND

ERISA is the primary federal law governing private sector pension plans, and includes requirements for plan sponsors to provide reports to agencies and disclosures to participants. Labor, PBGC, and IRS jointly interpret and clarify the provisions of ERISA that fall under their respective purviews through regulation and other guidance to help pension plan sponsors meet their responsibilities under the law.

Since ERISA was enacted in 1974, over 175,000 defined benefit (DB) plans have terminated, and defined contribution (DC) plans have replaced DB plans as the predominant type of pension plan. ERISA and related Internal Revenue Code (IRC) provisions have frequently been amended to reflect these and other developments. For example, the Pension Protection Act of 2006 (PPA) revised minimum plan funding standards, enhanced protections for spouses, strengthened plan asset diversification requirements, and included various provisions to improve the portability of pension plans, among other things.[6] These statutory changes have been accompanied by increases in the breadth and complexity of pension plan sponsors' reporting and disclosure requirements.

DB plans generally maintain a fund to provide a fixed level of monthly retirement income based on a formula specified in the plan. The employer is usually responsible for funding the plan, bears all the investment risk, and may be responsible for investing and managing its assets. In contrast, a DC plan does not promise a specific amount of benefits at retirement, but instead the benefit is based on the investment returns on employee and employer contributions to the employee's individual account. DC plan participants bear the full risk of investment and realize the gains and losses on those investments. DB and DC plans may be single-employer plans or they may be multiemployer plans, which are established through collective bargaining agreements including two or more employers and operated under the joint trusteeship of labor and management.[7]

Pension plans range considerably in terms of size: from one participant to several hundred thousand. The prevalence of plans in terms of type and size is illustrated in figure 1. Most plans are small (defined as fewer than 100 participants), thus small plans account for most report filings. However, since small plans have fewer participants, they are required to provide fewer disclosures.[8]

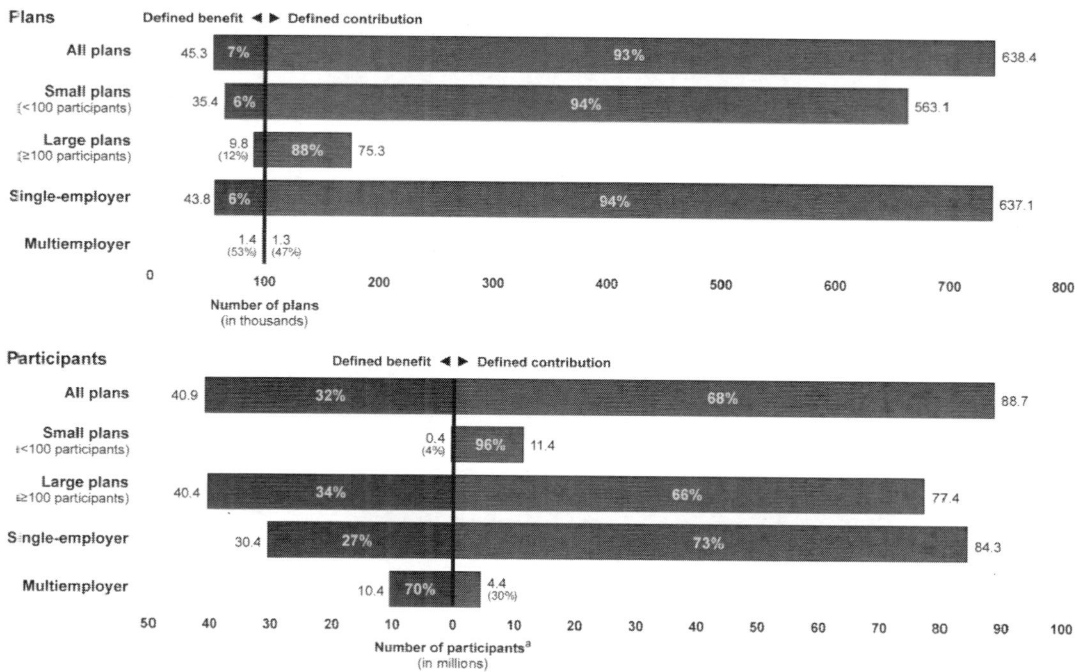

Source: GAO analysis of Labor's Abstract of 2011 Form 5500 Annual Reports, June 2013.

[a]Participant numbers cannot be totaled across plans because participants can be enrolled in more than one plan.

Figure 1. Number of Plans and Participants in Plans with Specific Characteristics, 2011.

Also, many more plans are single-employer than multiemployer, and they also represent many more participants, so the single-employer reporting and disclosure requirements apply to far more plans than the multiemployer reporting requirements. Reporting and disclosure tasks are frequently outsourced, in full or in part, to service providers such as accountants, actuaries, investment advisors and record keepers.

Labor, IRS, and PBGC each oversees a different aspect of private sector pension plans, with Labor taking primary responsibility for reporting and disclosure requirements. Labor promulgates regulations and produces other guidance related to reporting and disclosure. Within Labor, the mission of the Employee Benefits Security Administration includes ensuring work-related benefits and rights. Labor enforces requirements intended to ensure that pension plans operate in the best interest of participants and beneficiaries.[9]

IRS determines whether private sector pension plans qualify for preferential tax treatment under the IRC. Participants in tax-qualified pension plans can defer taxes on contributions and investment earnings until they receive benefits in retirement. In addition, contributions paid by an employer to or under a qualified pension plan are generally tax deductible as a business expense.[10] The IRC requires plan sponsors to submit certain reports in order to verify that plans meet certain of the criteria for tax-qualified status and to make certain disclosures to participants about retirement planning decisions for tax purposes. Title II of ERISA amended the IRC and included standards that plans must meet to qualify for preferential tax treatment.

PBGC insures the benefits of most private sector DB plan participants up to certain statutory limits in covered single-employer plans. When such plans terminate with insufficient assets to pay all benefits—as can happen in the bankruptcy of plan sponsors with underfunded plans—PBGC pays participants their benefits up to certain statutory limits. PBGC also provides assistance to multiemployer plans when such plans become insolvent. Accordingly, ERISA requires DB plan sponsors to pay premiums to insure plan benefits and provide information about the financial health of the plan. The information allows PBGC to focus resources on plans at risk of termination. PBGC reporting and disclosure is only required of DB plans that are insured by PBGC.[11] PBGC does not insure the benefits of participants in DC plans.

Three other federal agencies also have roles in pension reporting and disclosure requirements: the Social Security Administration (SSA), the Securities and Exchange Commission (SEC), and the Office of Management and Budget (OMB). SSA uses limited information about plan-vested beneficiaries to prepare notices to retirees about private sector pension benefits for which they may be eligible. SEC requires publicly-traded companies that permit employees to invest in employer stock in a voluntary contributory plan to file annual reports just as any such company offering stock, unless an exemption applies.[12] OMB, within the Executive Office the President, approves agency requests for information from the public, which includes private employers sponsoring retirement plans. OMB reviews the implementation of reporting requirements under the Paperwork Reduction Act of 1995,[13] to ensure that they involve only necessary information and do not impose an inordinate burden on those reporting.

REQUIRED REPORTS AND DISCLOSURES VARY BY PLAN TYPE, SIZE, AND CIRCUMSTANCES

To comply with the reporting and disclosure requirements specified under federal statute and regulation, Labor, IRS, and PBGC oversee more than 70 different reports and 60 different disclosures to participants that pension plan sponsors may have to provide, depending on their plans' type, size, and circumstances.[14] Some reports and disclosures are required to be provided on a routine basis, such as annually or quarterly, but most are nonroutine—that is, they are required to be provided on a one-time basis when some type of triggering event occurs. (See app. II for detailed lists of the reports and disclosures we identified.) Various reports and disclosures have been added over time through changes in statute and regulation, as a result of the development of new plan designs and in response to issues affecting participant security. For example, in 2002, following the scandal involving the Enron Corporation, a new disclosure requirement concerning periods when account activity is temporarily limited or restricted—referred to as blackout periods—was enacted by the Sarbanes-Oxley Act of 2002 to help protect pension participants in such situations.[15] In 2006, PPA also created several new disclosure requirements.[16] Other requirements, such as those related to the disclosure of fee and expense information by certain plans, were recently promulgated by regulation under ERISA.[17] A breakdown of the number of reports and disclosures under the purview of each federal agency is illustrated in figure 2. The system of reports and disclosures is complex, and determining which requirements may apply to any given plan can be challenging. Yet agency resources to help plan sponsors navigate this complex system are neither comprehensive nor up-to-date.

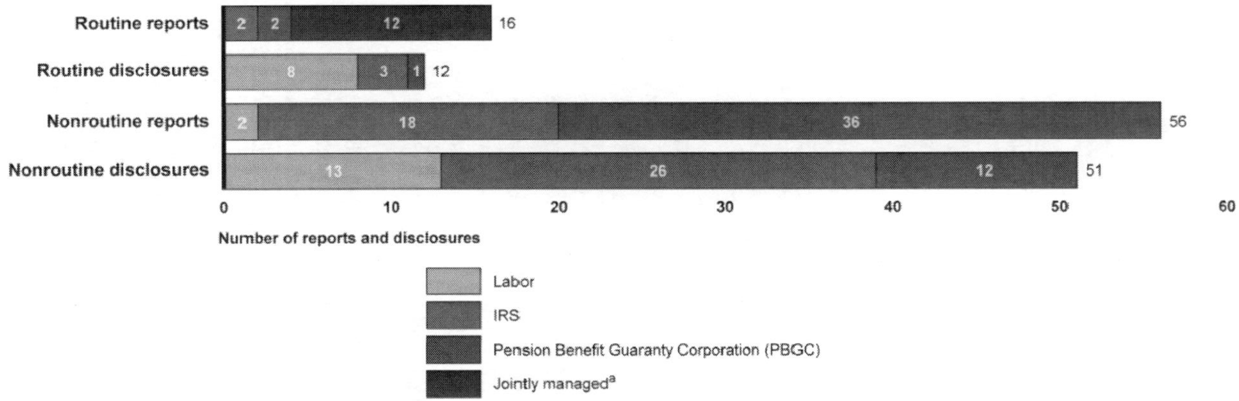

Source: GAO analysis of information provided by Labor, IRS, and PBGC, and related laws and regulations.
[a]The Form 5500 report and its schedules are jointly overseen by all three agencies.

Figure 2. Number of Routine and Nonroutine Reports and Disclosures by Lead Oversight Agency.

Routinely Required Reports and Disclosures Are Determined by Various Plan Characteristics

Virtually all plans are required to submit certain annual reports to the federal government and to send certain periodic disclosures to plan participants. For example, each year, most plan sponsors must submit a version of the Form 5500—the Form 5500 report, the 5500 short form (5500-SF), or the 5500 EZ—for each DB or DC plan they sponsor.[18] In plan year 2011, plan sponsors submitted more than 900,000 Form 5500, 5500-SF, and 5500 EZ reports combined. Most large plans with 100 or more participants file the Form 5500, while small plans covering fewer than 100 participants that are also invested in secure and easy to value assets may file the 5500-SF, and one-participant pension benefit plans and certain partnership and foreign plans may file the 5500-EZ. The forms call for varying levels of detailed information about participants, plan characteristics, and plan funding. Labor, IRS, and PBGC share the information reported in the Form 5500 and its attachments to help ensure that employee benefit plans are operated and managed in accordance with certain prescribed standards, and that participants, beneficiaries, and federal regulators have sufficient information to protect the rights and benefits of participants and beneficiaries under employee benefit plans. All large plans and many small plans must report their financial information on an attachment to their Form 5500: large plans must submit a schedule H and smaller plans may be required to submit a schedule I. Most small plans are eligible to file the Form 5500-SF, which contains a limited number of financial information fields in lieu of the schedule I.[19] Questions on the Form 5500, 5500-SF, and schedules H and I require sponsors to provide information on plan termination and transfers to other plans. In addition, all plans with benefits provided by an insurance company must also attach schedule A.[20] Some large plans have additional annual reporting requirements; those with loans or fixed income obligations in default or classified as uncollectible are required to attach schedule G.[21]

In addition, with limited exceptions, plan sponsors must provide participants in each DB and DC plan they sponsor three routine disclosures: the summary plan description (SPD), summary annual report or annual funding notice, and periodic pension benefit statement.[22] The SPD is the primary vehicle for informing participants and beneficiaries about their plan and how it operates, detailing information on when an employee can begin to participate in the plan, when benefits become vested, what the benefits are, and how to file a claim for benefits. The SPD must be provided to participants at least once every 10 years, or more often if there are changes, along with interim notices of any material changes in a "summary of material modification."[23] All plans, with limited exceptions, must provide to participants either the summary annual report or the annual funding notice, depending on their plan type. The summary annual report, required for DC plans, and DB plans in some instances, summarizes information from the Form 5500 and its attachments and includes a basic financial statement, minimum funding standards for plans, and participants' rights to other specific information. Most DB plans must file the annual funding notice, which provides participants with basic information about the plan's funding status and financial condition.[24] Pension benefit statements with information on benefits that have been accrued must also be provided periodically to all participants.[25] The specific contents and frequency of the benefit statements vary depending on the type of plan: individual account plans that permit participants and beneficiaries to direct the investment of assets in their account must provide a pension benefit statement at least once each calendar quarter, plans that do not provide participants or beneficiaries a right to direct their investments must provide the disclosure at least once each calendar year, and DB plans must provide it at least once every 3 years.

DB plans, which represent about 7 percent of all plans, are subject to additional reporting and disclosure requirements. For example, only DB plans must submit comprehensive premium filings to PBGC, with information requirements that vary according to plan size and funding level.[26] In addition, with limited exceptions, only DB plans must report their actuarial information on certain schedules attached to their Form 5500s.[27] DB plans have additional unique disclosure requirements. Certain DB plans must provide information through two additional annual disclosures: multiemployer plans must provide multiemployer pension plan summary plan information[28] and single-employer plans with more than one contributing sponsor not under common control must provide a notification to substantial employers.[29] Because DC plans are based on individual accounts, they are responsible for disclosures related to that characteristic. For example, only DC plans must inform participants of their right to make or change elective deferrals[30] and make an annual fee disclosure to their participants.[31]

DC plan sponsors may also make decisions in their plan design that create additional routine disclosure requirements. For example, to encourage participation, employers may enroll new employees automatically into their 401(k) plan.[32] The automatic enrollment plan design typically includes a default employee contribution rate and default investment arrangements, in which participants who have not specified their contributions or investments are assigned to a determined contribution level and selected investments.[33] Plan sponsors must inform participants of the automatic enrollment and defaults annually through two disclosures—the notice for fiduciary relief for investments in qualified default investment alternatives (QDIA)[34] and either the eligible automatic contribution arrangement (EACA) notice[35] or the qualified automatic contribution arrangements (QACA) notice.[36] The disclosures inform participants of the arrangements and their rights and options and participants may use the information to elect to change their contributions and investments or opt out of the arrangements. In addition, DC plans providing investment advice to participants through asset managers, such as a fiduciary advisor, must provide the notice of availability of investment advice to participants.[37]

To illustrate the variation in requirements, Table 1 describes the routine reports and disclosures required of DB and DC plans based on certain characteristics. Additional routine reports and disclosures may be required depending on a plan's specific design and circumstances. However, across the characteristics illustrated, the number of routine reports and disclosures that may be required ranges from seven to nine. For example, a small single-employer DB plan would be required to provide a total of seven routine reports and disclosures, while a large multiemployer DB plan would be required to provide a total of nine. Any DC plan would be required to provide a total of seven routine reports and disclosures, while those adopting an automatic enrollment design would be required to provide a total of nine.

Table 1. Variation in Required Routine Reports and Disclosures by Type, Size, and Design of Plan

	Name of report or disclosure
Defined benefit (DB) plans	
Reports required of all DB plans	Form 5500 OR 5500 short form OR 5500 EZ[a] Comprehensive premium filings to PBGC flat and variable rate
Additional reports based on type of DB plan	
If single-employer	5500 schedule SB
If multiemployer	5500 schedule MB[b] Zone status certification
Additional reports based on size of DB plan	
If large (100 or more participants)	5500 schedule H (financial information)
If large (500 or more participants)	Premium filings to PBGC estimated flat rate filing

Table 1. (Continued)

	Name of report or disclosure
If small (fewer than 100 participants)	5500 schedule I (financial information)[c]
Disclosures required of all DB plans	Periodic pension benefit statement Annual funding notice (or, in some cases, summary annual report) Summary plan description[d]
Defined contribution (DC) plans	
Reports required of all DC plans	Form 5500 OR 5500 short form OR 5500 EZ[a]
Additional reports based on size of DC plan	
If large (100 or more participants)	5500 schedule H
If small (fewer than 100 participants)	5500 schedule I[c]
Disclosures required of all DC plans	Periodic pension benefit statement Summary annual report Summary plan description[d] Effective opportunity to make or change elective deferrals Participant fee disclosure 404(a)
Additional disclosures based on certain DC plan designs	
If automatic enrollment (with default contribution and default investment arrangements)	Eligible automatic contribution arrangement notice (EACA) orQualified automatic contribution arrangement notice (QACA) Notice for fiduciary relief for investments in qualified default investment alternatives

Source: GAO analysis of information provided by Labor, IRS, and PBGC, and related laws and regulations.

Note: For this table, schedules of the 5500 are counted as separate reports. Additional routine reports and disclosures may be required if the plan meets additional criteria or under specific circumstances. See appendix II for additional details on routine and nonroutine reports and disclosures.

[a] A version of the Form 5500—the Form 5500 report, the 5500 short form (5500-SF), or the 5500 EZ— is required of most plans.

[b] Form 5500 schedule MB is required of certain defined contribution money purchase plans in addition to all multiemployer DB plans.

[c]Schedule I is not required of plans that file Form 5500 short form.

[d]The summary plan description is not required of certain types of plans (such as “top hat” plans and simplified employee pension plans) that meet the conditions for alternate method of compliance.

Nonroutine Reports and Disclosures Are Triggered by Certain Events

Beyond routine reporting and disclosure requirements, federal statutes and related regulations have also given rise to more than 100 different nonroutine reports and disclosures that may be required to be provided on a one-time basis when a specific triggering event or condition affects the plan or participant. In some cases, the conditions triggering a report or disclosure are fairly common, while other conditions are very rare. For example, one relatively common event is when a participant in a plan separates from employment with deferred vested benefits. In such cases, plan sponsors are required to file an annual registration statement identifying participants with deferred vested benefits (8955-SSA) with IRS and provide a disclosure to the separating participants about their benefits.[38] Another event that occurs fairly frequently is when a plan sponsor seeks a determination on the tax-qualified status of its plan from IRS. We identified six individual reports and one disclosure associated with such tax determination requests. IRS data indicate that plan sponsors submit at least 17,000 filings of these reports annually.

However, conditions that trigger most of the nonroutine reports and disclosures are relatively rare. Of the 40 nonroutine reports for which agencies provided data, only 5 had more than 5,000 filings in the most recent data year available.[39] Many (20) of the nonroutine reports for which data were reported had fewer than 100 filings. Several of the nonroutine reports with fewer than 100 reported filings are required of single-employer DB plans when an event occurs that might put plan benefits at risk, such as underfunding of the plan, bankruptcy, or distress termination. For example, each contributing sponsor of a single-employer DB plan, or a member of a contributing sponsor's controlled group, is required to submit an annual report of financial and actuarial information to PBGC (also known as the 4010) if the plan is less than 80 percent funded, could be subject to a lien, or still owe a portion of previously missed required contributions exceeding $1 million.[40] In fiscal year 2011, DB plan sponsors submitted 340 such reports.[41] In addition, 7 of the nonroutine reports may be required if the sponsor of a single-employer DB plan makes various changes, such as a change in plan ownership; none had more than 10 filings in fiscal year 2012.

Agencies Do Not Provide Clear and Comprehensive Information to Facilitate Compliance

Labor's mission includes efforts to ensure the security of Americans' retirement benefits by assisting and educating workers, plans sponsors, fiduciaries, and service providers, and by vigorously enforcing the law.[42] The need for such efforts is clear, especially with respect to helping plan sponsors navigate a complex system of more than 70 different reports and 60 different disclosures, and identify which they may be required to submit. Yet, the online resources provided by Labor and the other ERISA agencies to support plan sponsors in this process are not clear, comprehensive, or up-to-date.

As discussed above, a plan's type, size, and circumstances determine which routine reports and disclosures are required. Also, although many nonroutine reports and disclosures are limited to specific types of plans and are fairly rare, sponsors may find it challenging to recognize when their actions or circumstances have triggered the need for a report or disclosure. In addition, in some cases, reports and disclosures are subject to special requirements regarding to whom the information must be provided. For example, the annual funding notice—a routine report for all DB plans under Labor's purview—is required to be sent to PBGC, as well as to each plan participant and beneficiary, each labor organization representing such participants or beneficiaries and, in the case of multiemployer plans, to each employer that has an obligation to contribute to the plan.[43] Another example is the notification of resource benefit level—a nonroutine report triggered by insolvency in a multiemployer DB plan that does not terminate.[44] This report is required to be sent to PBGC, with copies to IRS, employers, employee organizations, participants, and beneficiaries. Adding to the complexity for many plan sponsors is the fact that they may sponsor more than one plan, so the burden of reporting is magnified. A plan sponsor may offer multiple plans of differing types and designs to employees. Alternatively, a sponsor may have stopped offering one type of plan and begun offering another—as with the shift from a DB to a DC plan, a growing trend over the past 3 decades—and as a result, may not be as familiar with the requirements applicable to the new plan type. In addition, even if a sponsor freezes a plan—that is, stops new employees from joining the plan, or stops previous employees from continuing to accrue benefits under the plan—certain reports and disclosures continue to be required until the plan terminates.[45]

In our efforts to identify required reports and disclosures, we found that each ERISA agency provides some online resources regarding these requirements. However, the resources provided are neither comprehensive nor up-to-date. They do not individually or as a whole provide sufficiently detailed, complete, up-to-date, and searchable information to allow plan sponsors to easily identify the reports and disclosures they must submit to be in compliance.

Labor's website provides the best information available from agencies through a guide listing many required reports and disclosures;[46] however, as we worked with the agencies to refine the list of reports and disclosures we had identified, we found that the guide was neither comprehensive nor fully accurate. To start, the guide is incomplete: it does not include many of the IRS reports and disclosures or several reports and disclosures under Labor's and PBGC's purview. Also, because the guide has not been updated since October 2008, it does not include recent reporting and disclosure requirements, such as the participant fee disclosure requirement, implemented in 2012. In addition, although the guide provides some information about the plan type that must report, to whom reports and disclosures must be provided, and citations to applicable federal laws, as well as available forms and model language and formats for some disclosures (referred to as "model notices"), this information is not systematic or comprehensive. Labor's guide does not always provide legal citations and, when provided, it does not list them consistently in the same place in the descriptions of each report and disclosure. Moreover, Labor's guide does not list all available model notices that might aid plan sponsors in compliance. For example, the guide does not indicate that there is a model for the annual funding notice or the notices of intent to terminate for standard and distress terminations.

PBGC's and IRS's websites also provide information on pension plan sponsors' reporting and disclosure requirements, including links to Labor's guide, but neither provides comprehensive information. For example, PBGC's website page on reporting and disclosure features certain selected requirements for DB plans, such as the annual funding notice, the annual report of financial and actuarial information (also known as the 4010), and other reportable events.[47] Other links to reports and disclosures are available on PBGC's website but they are not in a central location or easily searchable, which may make it difficult for plan sponsors to reliably determine if they have met all requirements. Similarly, IRS provides descriptions of certain selected reports and disclosures at several locations across its website. For example, the IRS site provides a page targeted to plan sponsors with brief descriptions of various reports that may be required,[48] and another page targeted to employees with rief descriptions of various disclosures that may be required.[49] However, these descriptions do not include information about the types of plans responsible for providing the reports and disclosures and the lists are not comprehensive.

Reports Involve Minimal Duplication, but Some Data Are Not Being Well-Managed

Minimal Duplication Reflects Agency Efforts to Eliminate Unnecessary Reporting

Our review of plan sponsor reports to agencies revealed only minimal redundancy, which was consistent with what we heard from associations we interviewed. We reviewed the content of routine reports that DC plans are required to submit annually or more frequently and found duplication only in plan identifying information and contact information for plan sponsors and administrators.

The general absence of duplication in reports to agencies may be due, in part, to the large portion of routine agency reporting subsumed by the Form 5500 annual report and its schedules, which are administered jointly by Labor, IRS and PBGC. By working together to develop the Form 5500 and its schedules, the three agencies can share the content and employee benefit plans can satisfy various annual reporting requirements under Title I and Title IV of ERISA and under the IRC. In addition, agency officials noted that representatives from all three agencies continue to meet regularly to look for opportunities to clarify and simplify the 5500 and its schedules.

Other efforts to eliminate unnecessary reporting by plan sponsors include actions taken under Executive Order 13,563, which calls on agencies to reduce their regulatory burden.[50] Both Labor and PBGC are considering actions that would reduce plan sponsor reporting requirements as a result of the order. For example, Labor is considering permitting certain individual account plans whose sponsors are in bankruptcy to file a summary terminal report instead of an annual Form 5500 report, which would allow plans to avoid costly annual audit fees that otherwise would diminish plan assets.[51] PBGC has also proposed new waivers that would allow some plans, identified as lower risk, to be exempt from certain reporting.[52] IRS officials described several initiatives under way in response to the executive order, but noted that none of these efforts are specifically focused on simplifying regulations related to pension reports and disclosures. All three agencies are also subject to the Paperwork Reduction Act, which requires that they manage information resources to reduce information collection burdens and obtain approval from OMB for their information collection requests.[53]

In general, plan sponsor representatives told us that they find the extent of duplication across reports to agencies to be minimal and not onerous. However, two associations and a service provider noted inconsistency between information reported on fees by service providers to sponsors[54] and information sponsors are required to report on the Form 5500 schedule C.[55] According to one industry representative, inconsistent definitions across the two reports result in vast differences in the content, making the service provider report less useful to plan sponsors as they prepare schedule C. Specifically, while both reports require information on service providers and indirect compensation, these terms are defined differently in the two reports. Labor officials explained that the service provider disclosure is prospective, to provide plan sponsors with fee information from service providers before entering into a contract. schedule C is retrospective, and provides information on the actual fees paid. Labor officials said the agency has received requests to change schedule C to better harmonize these requirements and is considering doing so.

Poorly Managed Data for One Report Results in Misleading Notices to Retirees

In our review of Labor's call center data,[56] we found that many participants were calling with questions about the potential private sector pension benefit information notice received from SSA,[57] which provides information about private pension benefits retirees may be owed by a past employer. The notices from SSA are based on data that plan sponsors are required to report to IRS, and we found that that poor management of the data, spread across three agencies, results in misleading information included in notices provided to some retirees.

Sponsors of plans that had participants separate from employment with deferred vested benefits are required to submit an annual report to the IRS: the registration statement identifying separated participants with deferred vested benefits, also known as the 8955-SSA.[58] IRS passes the information from the 8955-SSA to SSA. SSA then uses the data to inform retirees of the private pension benefits they may be entitled to when they apply for Social Security.[59]

The notice is intended to reflect all the deferred vested pension plan benefits claimants have earned from all previous employment in the private sector over the course of their careers, minus any distributions received. However, the vested benefits data are not managed in a way that ensures their accuracy. If retirees have questions about the benefits or need assistance, the notice instructs them to contact their plan administrator, previous employer, or Labor. A plan sponsor and an association we spoke with said such inquiries require investigations into plan records only to find, in some cases, that the benefits have already been distributed.[60]

According to industry representatives, inquiries regarding inaccurate notices of potential benefits that had actually already been paid can be burdensome and costly. Representatives of one plan sponsor said that they recently received an inquiry based on an SSA notice that took 16 hours to research because the record was from 1978. The plan sponsor representatives said the plan gets so many inquiries from retirees that it employs a full-time staff person at $60,000 per year to research potential benefits, and that the inquiries mean that the plan must retain participant benefit records in perpetuity. Officials from an association said that inquiries regarding potential benefits can create an administrative headache, even when no benefit is owed. They added that misreporting happens “a lot.”

We explored the reasons behind erroneous reports of potential benefits to retirees and found that decentralized administration, lack of data validation, unclear guidance, and paper reporting all create challenges to managing the data. Responsibility for the information is fragmented across three agencies: IRS, SSA, and Labor (see figure 3). The IRC requires plan sponsors to file the 8955-SSA reports with the IRS, but according to IRS officials, IRS does not use the data. As the statute requires, IRS passes the data along to SSA. SSA houses the data; eventually extracting individual records to send notices to retirees when they apply for Social Security. Finally, Labor is designated on the notice as the agency to contact for assistance, even though Labor is not involved in either the collection or maintenance of the data.[61] SSA officials noted that some participants need help from Labor to locate past employers when the employer contact information on the notice is outdated, which can often be the case due to mergers and acquisitions.[62] However, according to agency officials, none of these agencies ensures that the data are updated and accurate over time.

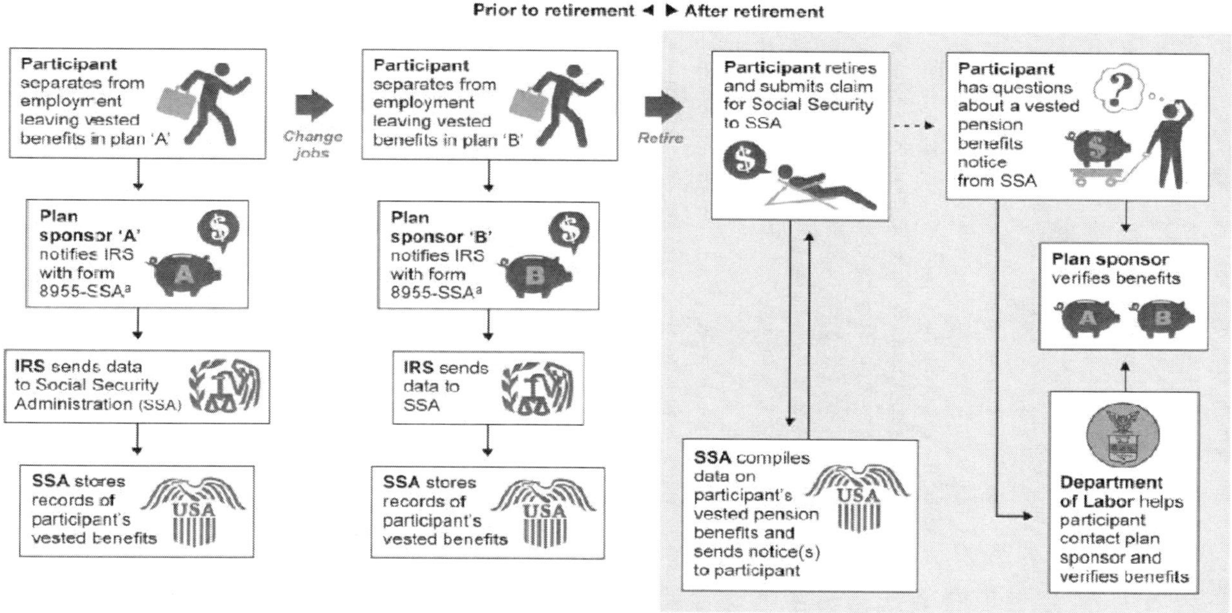

Source: GAO analysis of federal law, interviews with federal officials, and data on participant calls to benefits advisors at Labor.

[a]The plan sponsor is also required to provide participants with an individual statement, as required under 26 U.S.C. § 6057(e), at the time that form 8955-SSA notice is filed with IRS.

Figure 3. Fragmented Management of Data on Deferred Pension Benefits.

IRS simply collects and passes the data on to SSA. Rather than validate the accuracy of the data, SSA characterizes the information contained in its notices as describing potential pension plan benefits. Our review of Labor's call center data indicated that when participants called Labor about a potential benefit notice, benefits advisors often told participants the information was not reliable because the data are not regularly updated or verified and, in some cases, may be inaccurate.[63]

Unclear guidance is another factor that may be contributing to inaccurate data. We found the 8955-SSA instructions confusing, with seemingly conflicting guidance about whether participants with benefit payouts should be reported. One section of the 2012 instructions directs plan sponsors to identify distributions of benefits to previously-reported participants. Specifically, plan sponsors are directed to use a code to identify participants who were previously reported but are no longer entitled to deferred vested benefits, including participants receiving lump-sum payouts or participants transferred to another plan. However, the form's instructions also contain a section titled "When Not to Report a Participant" which instructs plan sponsors not to report participants who have been paid some or all of their deferred vested benefit. According to IRS officials, this part of the notice relates to when to report a participant for the first time; however, this may not be clear to some plan sponsors. In addition, in a meeting with employee benefits tax experts from eight different organizations, representatives of one association of certified public accountants told us that reporting distributions had not always been required. Although SSA would need such information to accurately update the data on benefits still owed over time, SSA officials said the IRS is the agency responsible for establishing the reporting requirements.

Excerpt of Potentially Confusing 2012 8955-SSA Instructions:

"When Not To Report a Participant

A participant is not required to be reported on Form 8955-SSA if, before the date of the Form 8955-SSA is required to be filed (including any extension of time for filing), the participant:

Is paid some or all of the deferred vested retirement benefit (See Caution below),

Returns to service covered by the plan and/or accrues additional retirement benefits under the plan, or

Forfeits all the deferred vested retirement benefit.

If payment of the deferred vested retirement benefit ceases before ALL of the participant's benefit is paid to the participant or beneficiary, information on the participant's remaining benefit shall be filed on the Form 8955-SSA filed for the plan year following the last plan year within which the payment ceased."

Source: 2011 Form 8955-SSA instructions.

In addition, plan sponsors are not required to submit the 8955-SSA electronically. Most submit it on paper, and some are handwritten, which may also contribute to inaccurate data. In 2012, SSA officials only received about 20 percent of the 8955-SSA submissions electronically from IRS. SSA officials estimated they will spend $668,000 in fiscal year 2013 processing the paper workload associated with the 8955-SSA, which includes paying a contractor to scan the documents into an electronic format. Data that cannot be scanned successfully are keyed in manually. Although electronic submissions could be less prone to data entry errors, as well as less costly to process, currently IRS is prohibited by statute from requiring that all sponsors submit information electronically, with limited exceptions.[64]

The importance of tracking an individual's pension benefits has grown as workers continue to have multiple jobs over the course of their careers. Each time an employee separates from employment, vested benefits may be left in the former employer's plan. As a result, over time, an individual may have accrued benefits that are left in several different plans.[65] The 8955-SSA is currently the only mechanism we identified for tracking a participant's retirement benefits earned over time and left in plans of various employers.

Despite the need for reliable benefit tracking, as long as management of the data remains fragmented, improvement in the accuracy of the data is unlikely. Beyond issuing the form and instructions, IRS views its role as merely to serve as a pass-through of the data from plan sponsors to SSA, SSA views its role as merely to provide retirees with whatever data they receive from IRS, and Labor views its role as merely to respond to inquiries. None voiced a willingness to assume responsibility for ensuring the accuracy of the data. As the agency that individuals contact when they are ready to retire, SSA may be the agency best situated to provide the notices to retirees about previously-earned private pension benefits. However, as the agency with primary responsibility for administering and enforcing private pension plans' reporting requirements under ERISA, we believe Labor may be best situated to provide consistent guidance and instruction, collect and maintain accurate data electronically, and respond to retiree inquiries on their benefits. Labor already administers a program to help participants track down their pension benefits. Under Labor's Abandoned Plan Program, the Employee Benefits Security Administration helps participants obtain their benefits when their plan lacks a responsible sponsor or administrator. In addition to Labor's program, PBGC maintains a database of missing participants with benefits in plans that have been terminated, and is in the process of expanding this program to include DC plans.[66]

LARGE NUMBER OF PARTICIPANT DISCLOSURES DO NOT ALWAYS COMMUNICATE EFFECTIVELY

The quantity of information that plan sponsors are required to disclose may be overwhelming and confusing to participants. We found that the content, presentation, and the grade-level at which disclosures are written may also present barriers to communication.[67] Concerns about the readability of participant disclosures are not new. In 2005 and again in 2009, the ERISA Advisory Council (EAC)[68] held hearings on the difficulties pension disclosures impose on both plan sponsors and participants.[69] Following the hearings in 2009, the EAC recommended improvements to individual participant disclosures and the system as a whole, including a recommendation that Labor review all pension plan disclosures required under Title I of ERISA to identify opportunities for streamlining. Although Labor agreed that disclosures would benefit from a comprehensive review, officials told us they had not yet implemented that recommendation.

Quantity of Information May Overwhelm Participants

Number of Disclosures Is Increasing

The breadth and complexity of pension plan sponsors' disclosure requirements have increased significantly since ERISA was enacted in 1974. As described earlier, our review identified more than 60 different disclosures to participants that pension plan sponsors may be required to provide, depending on their plans' type, size, and circumstances.

Within ERISA's overall reporting and disclosure framework, disclosures are intended to ensure that employee benefit plans are operated and managed in accordance with certain prescribed standards and that participants, beneficiaries, and regulators, have sufficient information to protect the rights and benefits of participants and beneficiaries under employee benefit plans. Thus, while some disclosures provide participants with information about their individual benefits, often disclosures also serve to hold plan fiduciaries to account for their actions.

Participants' calls to Labor focus on their individual benefits and retirement security. Plan sponsor disclosures that provide benefit information specific to a participant or provide information on what participant benefits are under the plan include the periodic pension benefit statement and the SPD. According to representatives of plan sponsors, associations, and participant advocacy groups we interviewed, these are the most useful and important types of disclosures for participants. They can help participants secure employer matching contributions to their 401(k) plans and help participants understand to what extent their benefits can fund their retirement. Such information can help participants obtain tax benefits or avoid tax penalties.[70] In contrast, disclosures mainly serving accountability purposes generally do not provide information specific to the retirement security of individual participants, focusing instead on aspects such as the funding or legal compliance of the plan as a whole.

Concerns Raised About Quantity of Disclosures

While requiring fiduciaries to disclose financial information about the plan may serve accountability purposes, as noted by a Labor official testifying before the EAC, the quantity of disclosures creates significant communication challenges as participants struggle with what they must or should read. For example, participants may receive a disclosure offering them an opportunity to comment on whether their plan should be tax-qualified, another notifying them that the plan has applied for a waiver of the minimum funding standard, and a summary annual report or annual funding notice providing annual plan-wide statistics. In addition, an academic researcher observed that participants do not understand what information is most relevant to their investment choices. Based on such testimony, the EAC concluded in 2009 that disclosures often go unread because participants feel overwhelmed by too much information.

Excerpt from the Model Notice of Application for a Waiver of the Minimum Funding Standard:

"This notice is to inform you that an application for a waiver of the minimum funding standard under § 412(d) of the Internal Revenue Code (Code) and section 303 of the Employee Retirement Income Security Act of 1974 (ERISA) has been submitted by *[INSERT PLAN SPONSOR'S NAME]* for the plan year beginning *[INSERT DATE*]. Under § 412(f)(4)(B) of the Code and section 303(e)(2) of ERISA, the Service will consider any relevant information submitted concerning this application for a waiver of the minimum funding standard. You may send this information to the following address..."

Source: IRS Internal Revenue Bulletin 2004-07.

Our interviews with various group echoed these concerns. One participant advocate said participants are being "flooded" with information from their plans, and an association representative commented that there is too much information for it to be useful to participants. A service provider noted that at retirement, participants get at least 20 pieces of paper, which is too much information to read and act on. According to several groups we spoke with, the quantity of information diminishes the positive effects it can have for participants. Service providers and associations said participants may miss important information because they have to read through such a large quantity of other content to find it, and many participants rarely read the disclosures they receive. Furthermore, Labor officials noted that, although some plan sponsors pay all the expenses of their plans, the cost of participant disclosures in DC plans is often paid from participant accounts through added direct fees or indirect charges to plan investments. One association commented that participants would not want to receive all the currently mandated disclosures if they understood they were paying for them.

Limited Efforts to Streamline Disclosure Requirements

The agencies have taken some steps to facilitate the consolidation of disclosures. For example, in 2007 Labor and IRS worked together to develop a model notice to assist plan sponsors to comply with four disclosure requirements in a single, stand-alone document.[71] However, such examples are rare. In our review we found several instances of nearly identical statements appearing in multiple disclosures. The participant benefit statement, the disclosure of plan fees and expenses, and the QDIA are all required to contain explanations of limitations on the rights of participants to direct investments. Similar statements about plan funding appear in both the annual funding notice and the notice of critical or endangered status.[72] The SPD, required of most DB and DC plans, generally includes a description of eligibility requirements, benefits, and circumstances in which benefits may be reduced, while other disclosures also contain similar information. But, in other cases, the information in disclosures is fairly unique. For example, we reviewed selected disclosures from samples provided by a plan sponsor organization, comparing the content of two disclosures provided to employees when they separate from employment with six disclosures that are provided routinely to all participants once they join a plan, and we found minimal overlap across these disclosures.

Another way that disclosures can be consolidated is by combining them in a single mailing. Labor and IRS officials said they generally allow disclosures to be combined in a single mailing. However, plan sponsors may find the guidance is unclear. According to one service provider, there is no explicit, broadly applicable guidance encouraging the practice when disclosure schedules align, and current industry practice is to keep them separate. Certain nonroutine disclosures cannot be combined for practical purposes, as they are timed to coincide with a triggering event that may not coincide with another mailing. Moreover, in one case, combining disclosures is expressly discouraged. The preamble to the final QDIA notice regulations states that if the QDIA notice were combined with the SPD, the length and complexity of SPDs might lead to participants missing the QDIA information. According to Labor officials it is not clear that participants benefit from receiving a large quantity of information all at once. As noted above, the quantity of content participants receive can be overwhelming and cause participants to miss important information because there is so much to read.

Nevertheless, agencies could make further efforts to streamline disclosures. For example, we previously recommended that Congress consider consolidating the annual funding notice and the notice of critical or endangered status to eliminate duplication.[73] One association representative we spoke with noted that agencies could provide regulatory relief to sponsors by allowing them to refer participants to the SPD for information, as is already done to some extent, rather than repeating it in various disclosures.

Participants Often Lack Basic Information

While participants may receive a large quantity of content from their plans, our review of Labor's call center data indicates that many participants call with basic questions about their rights to benefits. Much of this information is included in the plan's SPD. In a framework of disclosures intended to help participants protect their rights and benefits under their plans, the SPD is required to explain those rights and benefits. Labor described the content of the SPD, along with the relevant summary of the material modifications, to OMB in 2013 as the single most important source of information about a plan for the plan participants.[74]

Plan sponsors are required to provide SPDs to participants when they initially join the plan, but then plan sponsors are only required to provide SPDs again to participants every 5 years if the plan has changed, or 10 years if the plan has not changed.[75] Also, unlike parts of DB plan annual reports, the SPD is not required to be posted to plan sponsor intranet sites.[76] As a result, if participants have questions and cannot find their SPDs, Labor's benefits advisors must first help participants obtain a copy of their SPDs by advising participants to mail a certified letter to their plan administrator requesting one, and occasionally contacting employers on their behalf.[77]

The rollover notice, with information on distribution options, conveys information that is important for participants to have, especially when deciding whether to take a distribution from their plans. However, participants may not be receiving timely access to this information. As we recently reported, IRS regulations do not require plans to provide the requisite distribution information when a participant separates from employment, but rather within a specified window of time before the receipt of a distribution. We identified no requirements to ensure that participants receive timely information on their distribution options before they make a decision to take a distribution.[78]

Disclosures Are Often Confusing

ERISA's and IRC's disclosure requirements often specify that notices be written in a manner calculated to be understood by the average participant (see app. III). For other disclosures without this specific language about readability in the underlying statute, Labor officials noted that ERISA's basic fiduciary standards would also require that plan sponsors consider how understandable participant disclosures are as part of their fiduciary duty.[79] Nevertheless, our review found that disclosures often contain complex content and are difficult to understand. The complexity of disclosures varies, and some model notices also fall short. According to agency officials, ERISA agencies do little to enforce the statutes' readability provisions.

Complexity of Disclosures Varies

While complex information is required to be included in the disclosures in many cases by statute, the readability of disclosures also depends, in part, on how the plan sponsor writes them. Representatives of one plan sponsor we spoke with said they use field tests and polls to determine whether their communication with participants is effective, and they strive to write disclosures at an eighth-grade reading level. A participant advocacy group representative commented that some plan administrators definitely do a better job than others in terms of the readability of their disclosures. However, representatives from two participant advocacy groups we interviewed told us that the content of certain disclosures is confusing for participants. For example, one group commented that some notices are written in language that even lawyers cannot understand. A service provider we interviewed commented that although the model blackout notice (a nonroutine disclosure that may be triggered for DC plans) is seven paragraphs long, sponsors should be able to communicate its content in only three or four sentences. To gain some insight on participant perspectives, we also analyzed calls participants made to Labor's call center during fiscal year 2012. We found that participants often had questions because they did not understand the content of a disclosure or why it was sent to them. Some callers stated that they did not know how to interpret a disclosure and were frustrated or alarmed, suspecting their benefits might be in jeopardy.

Table 2 summarizes some of the comments made in our interviews with plan sponsor representatives and participant advocacy groups, in participant calls to Labor, and in EAC reports about the challenges related to three disclosures that were frequently mentioned: the summary annual report, the annual funding notice, and the notice of an IRS request for determination.

Table 2. Comments on Disclosures Identified as Difficult to Understand

Disclosure	Description	Selected comments about challenges with disclosures
Summary annual report	Among other plan information, the summary annual report provides DC and some DB plan participants the total assets, income, expenses, and the number of participants in the plan.	•Witnesses before an EAC working group in 2005 said that the text format of the summary annual report is an

Table 2. (Continued)

Disclosure	Description	Selected comments about challenges with disclosures
		ineffective way to present financial data, and that the disclosure should be eliminated if it is not redesigned to be more useful and informative.
Annual funding notice	This notice provides DB plan participants with actuarial data about the plan's funding, including the plan's funding target attainment percentage (FTAP) for the last 3 years and general information about the benefits guaranteed by the PBGC. The notice provides statements on the plan's credit balance and detailed information about how the plan's assets are invested.	•Representatives from an association of actuaries told us the notice is largely not read or not understood, andonly a few of the numbers in the notice could conceivably be useful. •A participant called Labor's call center saying he received this notice regarding the Pension Protection Act of 2006 and wanted to know if he had lost his benefits.
Notice to interested parties of application for advanced determination regarding the qualifications of a plan under the IRC	This notice provides DC and DB plan participants an opportunity to comment on whether their plans meet requirements in the IRC. It can be provided with respect to a plan's initial qualification, amendment, termination, or partial termination.	•According to Labor benefits advisors, participants are often confused by this notice. •IRS officials said they sometimes get responses about multiemployer plans from labor organizations, rather than individual participants. •Labor officials commented that the complex nature of tax qualification requirements make it difficult for the average pension plan participant to exercise this right.

Source: Agency documents, Interviews with officials at federal agencies and an association, participant call data, and the 2005 EAC Report of the Working Group on Communications to Retirement Plan Participants.

Some Agency Model Notices Fall Short

Labor, PBGC, and IRS have created templates (referred to as "model notices") for plan sponsors to follow when writing all or a portion of certain disclosures to assist them in complying with the law.[80] While plan sponsors are not required to use model notices, those testifying before the EAC, as well as various groups we spoke with, indicated that model notices are widely used and helpful to both plans sponsors and participants.[81] Thus, to further evaluate the readability of disclosures to participants, we assessed the extent to which ten of these model notices adhered to the federal plain language guidelines—a handbook federal agencies are encouraged to use when communicating with the public.[82] We found that several of the model notices failed to meet criteria we developed based on these guidelines, more often than not.[83] For example:

Excerpt from the Model Rollover Notice:

"If you do not do a direct rollover, you may still do a rollover by making a deposit into an IRA or eligible employer plan that will accept it. You will have 60 days after you receive the payment to make the deposit. If you do not do a direct rollover, the Plan is required to withhold 20% of the payment for federal income taxes (up to the amount of cash and property received other than employer stock). This means that, in order to roll over the entire payment in a 60-day rollover, you must use other funds to make up for the 20% withheld. If you do not roll over the entire amount of the payment, the portion not rolled over will be taxed and will be subject to the 10% additional income tax on early distributions if you are under age 591/2 (unless an exception applies)."

Source: IRS, Notice 2009-68.

- **Explain technical terms:** Several model notices use technical terms without explanation, and several require the reader to cross-reference other sources of information to understand the main ideas. For example, the notice of IRS request for determination invites participants to comment on whether their plan meets requirements in sections 401 and 403(a) of the IRC without further explanation of those citations.
- **Specify whether action is needed or advised:** Several model notices do not make it clear what the participant is supposed to do with the information. The model rollover disclosure gives participants the

general idea that they are to use the seven pages of information to help decide whether to roll over their retirement funds. However, it does not state clearly and up front that for tax purposes, in most circumstances, participants under 591/2 should not withdraw their retirement funds, and after that age participants should take distributions only a little at a time. Participants need to infer that from other information the disclosure provides.

- **Offer help for non-English speakers:** None of the model notices we reviewed contain language about assistance available to non-English speakers.[84] This includes the model notice for the summary annual report, which is required by ERISA to provide assistance to non-English speakers when enough non-English speakers participate in the plan.[85]

Finally, we also tested the model notices we identified with an automated grade-level readability test.[86] According to the test, the reading level required for the models ranged from that of a tenth-grader to that of a college senior. Most were written above a high-school reading level (see table 3).[87] Thus, it seems likely that the information in these disclosures would not be readily understandable to many average plan participants and that readability might present a challenge for participants, even when plan sponsors adopt the model notice developed by the agency.

Table 3. Grade-Level Reading Scores for Model Notices

Disclosure	Source of model notice	Grade-levelreading score
Blackout notice	Labor: 29 C.F.R. § 2520.101-3(e)(2)	15.7
ERISA rights statement	Labor: 29 C.F.R. § 2520.102-3(t)(2)	15.5
Notice to interested parties of IRS determination	IRS: Revenue Procedure 2011- 06	14.8
Notice of pending election of multiemployer status	Labor: Model Notice of Pending Election of Multiemployer Plan Status, 71 Fed. Reg. 69,595 (Dec. 1, 2006)	14.9

Disclosure	Source of model notice	Grade-levelreading score
Diversification requirements for qualified defined contribution plans holding publicly traded employer securities	IRS: Notice 2006-107	14.8
Rollover notice	IRS: Notice 2009-68	14.4
Saver's credit notice[a]	IRS: Announcement 2001-106	14.2
Critical status notice	Labor: Model Notice of Multiemployer Plan in Critical Status, 73 Fed. Reg. 15,692 (Mar. 25, 2008)	14.0
Annual funding notice[b]	Labor: Field Assistance Bulletin 2009-01[b]	13.4
Notice of application to waive the minimum funding standard	IRS: Bulletin 2004-7 Appendix A	15.1
Summary annual report	Labor: 29 C.F.R. § 2520.104b-10(d)(3)	12.3
Notice of intent to terminate (distress termination)	PBGC: Appendix B to PBGC distress termination instructions	11.1
Notice of termination of individual account plan	Labor: 29 C.F.R. § 2550.404a-3 Appendix	11.2
Notice related to qualified automatic contribution arrangements, eligible automatic contribution arrangements, and qualified default investment alternatives.	IRS: Website (http://www.irs.gov/pub/irs-tege/sample_notice.pdf)	10.9
Notice of intent to terminate (standard termination)	PBGC: Appendix B to PBGC standard termination instructions	10.4
Model comparative chart on investment options	Labor: 29 C.F.R. § 2550. 404a-5 Appendix	9.7

Sources: Agency regulations and guidance, as cited above, and GAO analysis using the Flesch-Kincaid Grade-Level (FKGL) tool. (For more information on this tool and our analysis, see app. I.)

[a]IRS Announcement 2001-106 encourages employers to tell their employees about this available tax credit, and offers the model notice as an option to accomplish that. The notice is not required to be provided by law.

[b]Labor has proposed a new model for this disclosure (75 Fed. Reg. 70,625, Nov. 18, 2010). Although the regulations with this new model have not yet been finalized, Labor officials noted that plan sponsors could use this model, if they wish.The FKGL score for this revised notice is slightly lower: 12.8.

Readability Provisions Are Not Vigorously Enforced

An additional challenge to participant disclosure understandability is that Labor, IRS, and PBGC do not vigorously enforce the readability standards in ERISA or the IRC. We identified 11 disclosures that are required by ERISA or the IRC to be understandable by an average plan participant (see app. III). However, agency officials said their agencies had not issued any guidance, other than the model notices, on how to comply with these standards.

One of the recommendations of the EAC in 2005 was to enhance or create mechanisms to enforce the regulatory requirement that the SPD be understandable by the average plan participant. For that disclosure, if Labor investigates a plan, officials said that investigators will consider whether the plan's SPD is in compliance with ERISA readability standards. Similarly, IRS officials said that if a plan is audited and the examiner reads a notice and cannot tell what it says, that might be noted in the audit. In addition, according to Labor officials, disclosure readability is in part addressed through public comments on proposed regulations. Labor officials said that sometimes readability can be improved with information collected through the focus groups that Labor increasingly conducts during the rulemaking process.[88] IRS officials said they also try to make model notices readable, and that model notices are very closely vetted on a word-by-word basis. At the same time, they noted that the complexity of the content that disclosures are often required by statute to contain can make them difficult to read, even when the IRC requires that they be understandable by the average plan participant. PBGC officials said that they are working with Labor to make some content in the model annual funding notice more understandable, but that the statutory requirements for the content in the notice place limitations, in effect, on its readability.

Nevertheless, all three ERISA agencies acknowledged that enforcing the specific readability standards in the statutes is not a priority, and none had a mechanism to determine whether disclosures are understandable to an average participant.

CONCLUSION

The increasingly complex world of private sector pension plans, coupled with the important role these plans play in the retirement security of millions of Americans, has made access to clear information about plan details more important than ever. Agencies use information from plan sponsors for oversight purposes, while participants need access to plan information to manage their retirement accounts and make key retirement decisions. Therefore, enhancing plan sponsor compliance and the efficiency and effectiveness of reports and disclosures is of the utmost importance.

Retirees with vested benefits in a former employer's plan could receive more accurate and up-to-date information if responsibility for collecting and managing information on participants' deferred vested benefits was more centralized. The current system splits the responsibility for collecting this information (assigned to IRS) from the responsibility for retaining that information (assigned to SSA), but leaves Labor responsible for helping plan participants understand and follow up on notices with this information. With no agency fully responsible for the data throughout this process, individuals with vested benefits in former employers' plans may continue to receive outdated information. As the agency with primary responsibility for administering and enforcing pension plan reporting requirements under ERISA, Labor may be best situated to take on this responsibility, perhaps in partnership with PBGC, given that agency's expanded role in maintaining a database of plans' missing participants.

The increased complexity of retirement plans and the vast financial resources they contain necessitates a complex system of reporting and disclosures to ensure oversight and transparency. Plan sponsors do not need to understand the details of reporting and disclosure requirements for which they are not responsible, but they must have sufficient information to determine which requirements apply to them. Currently, there is no single comprehensive and regularly updated resource to help sponsors comply with reporting and disclosure requirements. Providing sponsors with a well-organized and complete guide would promote compliance and help ensure that agencies and participants receive the required information when needed.

For participants, understanding their rights and benefits, as provided in the SPD for their plan, is crucial to safeguarding and managing their retirement security. Currently, plan sponsors are required to provide participants with the SPD once every 5 years if the plan has changed, or 10 years if the plan has not changed.

In the intervening time, participants may have difficulty finding the information, as updates may be provided intermittently through summaries of material modifications. Many plan sponsors already provide plan information to participants securely through dedicated intranet sites. Requiring plan sponsors to include the SPD and any summaries of material modifications on such a site would provide participants continuous access to plan details.

Finally, participants must understand disclosures to use the information to protect their rights and benefits. The complex nature of retirement plans and the detailed information that plan sponsors are required to disclose may make ERISA's readability requirements challenging for plan sponsors to meet and for agencies to enforce.

Thus, although Congress included many provisions in ERISA and in the IRC requiring that disclosures be written so that the average plan participant can understand them, Labor, IRS, and PBGC officials acknowledged that enforcement of these provisions has not been a priority. Setting clear criteria for statutory readability standards, enforcing them, and revising model notices as appropriate may help ensure that, in the future, disclosures are clearer and easier to read for participants who are trying to manage their accounts to better secure their retirement.

Furthermore, such measures may also reduce the costs associated with Labor's benefits advisors responding to participant questions.

Matter for Congressional Consideration

To increase the accuracy of "potential private pension benefit information" notices that SSA sends to Social Security claimants, Congress should consider legislation shifting responsibility and necessary resources to Labor for (a) electronically collecting form 8955-SSA information on participants' deferred vested benefits, (b) maintaining an accurate federal database of those benefits, and (c) periodically sending SSA accurate information about such benefits for recent Social Security claimants identified by SSA, so that SSA may provide notices to retirees.

RECOMMENDATIONS FOR EXECUTIVE ACTION

To ease the burden on plan sponsors, enhance compliance, and help ensure that disclosures to participants are written in a manner that can be understood by the average participant, Labor, IRS, and PBGC should work together to:

1) Create and regularly update a comprehensive online tool for plan sponsors to search for the reports and disclosures they are required to provide based on plan type, design, and circumstances.
2) Define criteria for complying with the readability provisions in ERISA and the IRC, and apply the criteria to agency-generated model notices as well as those developed by plan sponsors. As part of these criteria, consider requiring clear, simple, brief highlights at the beginning of disclosures, reflecting federal plain language guidelines.

   To better ensure plan participants have access to information about their rights and benefits, as currently in force under their plans, Labor should:
3) Direct plan sponsors to post to any intranet website maintained by the employer, as soon as determined feasible by Labor, a copy of the most current summary plan description (SPD) and any summary of material modifications issued subsequent to that SPD.

AGENCY COMMENTS AND OUR EVALUATION

We provided a draft of this report to the Department of Labor, Department of the Treasury and Internal Revenue Service, Pension Benefit Guaranty Corporation, and Social Security Administration for review. All the agencies generally agreed with our report.

Labor and Treasury/IRS provided similar comments regarding our first recommendation, agreeing to work together with PBGC to explore the necessity and viability of providing a comprehensive online tool that would enable plan sponsors to search for required reports and disclosures based on plan type, design, and circumstances. In technical comments, Labor noted that the agency expects to publish an updated version of its reporting and disclosure guide for employee benefit plans soon. We appreciate Labor's and Treasury/IRS' efforts and believe that a well-designed and searchable tool would be invaluable to the broad sponsor community.

Labor and Treasury/IRS also provided similar comments regarding our second recommendation, to define criteria for complying with the readability provisions of ERISA and the IRC. They agreed that the subject matter of disclosures can be complicated, noting that they have increased the use of model notices to provide plan sponsors and participants with clear and understandable formats for complying with applicable requirements. However, Labor also noted that plan sponsors have expressed concern regarding liabilities that may result from ambiguities that arise when complex information is summarized or presented using plain language criteria. We agree. It is for this reason our recommendation calls for clear, simple, brief highlights to be added to— not replace—full disclosures. Such highlights could help plan sponsors comply with the provisions in ERISA and IRC that require certain disclosures to be understandable to the average plan participant, while not compromising the complex information that the disclosures must contain. Treasury/IRS also expressed interest in directing plan sponsors to use certain plain language guidelines to make disclosures more understandable.

Regarding our third recommendation, to direct plan sponsors who have intranet sites for their plans to post the most current summary plan description and any subsequent summaries of material modifications to these sites Labor noted that, in 2011, it published a request for information to explore whether and how to modify disclosure standards, taking into account current technology. Labor pointed out that ERISA was previously amended to include actuarial information and agreed to consider the benefit of such an intranet posting with respect to the summary plan description and material modifications. However, Labor also noted that it is unclear whether the agency has the statutory authority to require such online posting. We would encourage Labor to fully consider what actions it could take within the scope of its existing authority.

Treasury/IRS also provided comments on the matter for congressional consideration, which asks Congress to consider legislation shifting responsibility and resources to Labor for collecting, maintaining, and periodically sending SSA the information reported on the 8955-SSA. Treasury/IRS noted that the agency is considering regulatory changes to help address the problem of participants receiving notices from SSA describing vested benefits that have already been paid. To improve the accuracy of data, the agency has issued proposed regulations that would require the 8955-SSA to be filed electronically, to the extent allowable under the current law, and the agency is working on a project, listed in its 2013-2014 priority guidance plan, that would allow the 8955-SSA to satisfy the requirement that sponsors provide an annual participant disclosure of separated participants with deferred vested benefits. While we applaud these efforts to improve the accuracy of 8955-SSA data, we remain concerned that such efforts only address part of the problem. The data from the 8955-SSA must also be maintained and updated over time to produce accurate notices once individuals are ready to retire. We continue to believe that it would be preferable to more fully centralize responsibility for collecting and maintaining these data and that Labor, perhaps in partnership with PBGC, may be best situated to assume responsibility for these tasks.

PBGC commented more generally that pension law is highly prescriptive and ERISA agencies could implement the results of their cooperative efforts more effectively if they were given more discretion under the law.

Each agency also provided technical comments, which we incorporated as appropriate.

Charles A. Jeszeck, Director
Education, Workforce,
and Income Security Issues

Appendix I: Methodology for Analyzing the Readability of Participant Disclosures

To analyze the readability of participant disclosures, we evaluated the language in model disclosures developed by the Department of Labor (Labor) and the Internal Revenue Service (IRS) with both an automated readability tool and criteria based on federal plain language guidelines for communicating with the public. Although we found no comprehensive list of existing model notices, we identified 16 such notices through our review of laws and regulations.[1]

To estimate the reading level at which model disclosures were written, we evaluated the language in the 16 model disclosures we identified using the Flesch-Kincaid Grade-Level (FKGL) automated readability tool. The FKGL tool was developed by the Navy based on the Flesch Reading Ease test, which is one of the most widely-used, tested, and reliable formulas for calculating readability. The FKGL tool was developed primarily for adults and has been tested extensively on adult materials. It uses core measures of word length and sentence length to estimate the grade level at which the content is written. The version we used was included in the word processing software Microsoft Word. We deleted parenthetical instructions to plan sponsors from the models before we ran the analysis to focus on the readability of content intended for participants.

To evaluate model disclosure readability more generally, we developed 22 criteria based on federal plain language guidelines for communicating with the public.[2]

The federal plain language guidelines is a handbook that federal agencies are encouraged to use when communicating with the public. We distilled the guidelines into 22 criteria on factors such as the organization and presentation of the content. Two GAO analysts independently coded 10 model notices on the 22 criteria and assessed whether the disclosures would be understandable to an average plan participant.[3] When coding differences occurred, a third GAO analyst independently reviewed those cases and discussed with the team to reach agreement.

APPENDIX II: REQUIRED PENSION PLAN REPORTS AND DISCLOSURES

To determine what reports and disclosures private sector pension plan sponsors are required to make to federal agencies and plan participants, respectively,[1] we compiled previously-available lists and other information about reports and disclosures from agency websites and lists from three service provider websites.

The assembled information included details about who must submit information, to whom it must be provided, citations to federal laws, regulations, and guidance, available forms and model notices, and events and circumstances that trigger reports and disclosures. We then worked with officials at the agencies—Labor, IRS, and PBGC—to revise and update the list and add details about reports and disclosures through multiple steps. We then reviewed relevant federal statutes and regulations to verify selected information. These lists have been summarized below into four tables: routine reports; nonroutine reports, routine disclosures, and nonroutine disclosures.

Table 5. Plan Sponsors' Routine Reports to Agencies

Name of routine report (to be provided annually unless noted otherwise)	Agency providing oversight and primary recipient	Plans required to provide report	Applicable laws, regulations, and agency guidance	Form
Annual return/report Form 5500[a]	Labor, PBGC, and IRS	Defined benefit (DB) and defined contribution (DC) plans	•26 U.S.C. §§ 6047(e), 6057(b) and 6058(a). •29 U.S.C. §§ 1024 and1365. •29 C.F.R. § 2520.103-1.	Form 5500 submitted electronically using EFAST2system. Extension obtained by filing form 5558 with IRS or by automatic extension by extending corporate tax return with IRS.
Annual return/report 5500-SF (short form)	Labor, PBGC, and IRS	DB and DC small plans covering fewer than 100 participants that are 100% invested in "secure" and "easy to value" assets. Certain "one-participant plans" are permitted to file electronically the Form 5500-SF in lieu of filing the Form 5500-EZ on paper with the IRS	•26 U.S.C. §§ 6057(b) and 6058(a). •29 U.S.C. §§ 1024 and 1365.	5500-SF submitted electronically using EFAST2system. Extension obtained by filing form 5558 with IRS or by automatic extension by extending corporate tax return with IRS

Table 5. (Continued)

Name of routine report (to be provided annually unless noted otherwise)	Agency providing oversight and primary recipient	Plans required to provide report	Applicable laws, regulations, and agency guidance	Form
Annual return/report form 5500-EZ	IRS	DB and DC plans (small one-participant pension benefit plans. It may also be used by certain partnership plans and certain foreign plans)	•26 U.S.C. § 6058(a).	Form 5500-EZ must be filed by paper and mail to IRS. However, one-participant plans may satisfy their filing obligations under Code by filing Form 5500-SF electronically under EFAST2 system, if certain conditions are met
Annual return/report (5500) attachments (e.g. financial statements, and accountant's opinions)	Labor, PBGC, and IRS	DB and DC plans as required in form 5500	•29 U.S.C. § 1023(a)(3).	No form (attachments to Form 5500)

Name of routine report (to be provided annually unless noted otherwise)	Agency providing oversight and primary recipient	Plans required to provide report	Applicable laws, regulations, and agency guidance	Form
Annual return/report (5500) schedule A—insurance information	Labor, PBGC, and IRS	DB and DC large plans (100 or more participants) with benefits provided by an insurance company	•29 U.S.C. §§ 1023(a)(2) and 1024.	Form 5500 schedule A submitted electronically using EFAST2 system. Extension obtained by filing form 5558 with IRS or by automatic extension by extending corporate tax return with IRS
Annual return/report (5500) schedule C—service provider information	Labor, PBGC, and IRS	DB and DC plans with service providers who rendered services to the plan or direct filing entity (DFE) during the plan or DFE year, received $5,000 or more in compensation from the plan	•29 U.S.C. § 1024.	Form 5500 schedule C submitted electronically using EFAST2 system. Extension obtained by filing form 5558 with IRS or by automatic extension by extending corporate tax return with IRS

Table 5. (Continued)

Name of routine report (to be provided annually unless noted otherwise)	Agency providing oversight and primary recipient	Plans required to provide report	Applicable laws, regulations, and agency guidance	Form
Annual return/report (5500) schedule D—DFE/participating plan information	Labor, PBGC, and IRS	DB and DC plans or direct filing entities (DFE) that invested or participated in certain financial instruments	•29 U.S.C. § 1024.	Form 5500 Schedule D-DFEsubmitted electronically using EFAST2 system. Extension obtained by filing form 5558 with IRS or by automatic extension by extending corporate tax return with IRS
Annual return/report (5500) schedule G—financial transaction schedules	Labor, PBGC, and IRS	DB and DC large plans (100 or more participants) with loans or fixed income obligations in default or classified as uncollectible	•26 U.S.C. § 6058(a). •29 U.S.C. § 1024.	Form 5500 Schedule G submitted electronically using EFAST2 system. Extension obtained by filing form 5558 with IRS or by automatic extension by extending corporate tax return with IRS

Name of routine report (to be provided annually unless noted otherwise)	Agency providing oversight and primary recipient	Plans required to provide report	Applicable laws, regulations, and agency guidance	Form
Annual return/report (5500) schedule H—large plan financial information	Labor, PBGC, and IRS	DB and DC large plans (100 or more participants)	•26 U.S.C. § 6058(a). •29 U.S.C. § 1024.	Form 5500 Schedule H submitted electronically using EFAST2 system. Extension obtained by filing form 5558 with IRS or by automatic extension by extending corporate tax return with IRS
Annual return/report (5500) schedule I—small plan financial information	Labor, PBGC, and IRS	DB and DC small plans (fewer than 100 participants and filing the Form 5500 annual return/report, rather than the Form 5500-SF)	•26 U.S.C. § 6058(a). •29 U.S.C. § 1024.	Form 5500 Schedule I submitted electronically using EFAST2 system. Extension obtained by filing form 5558 with IRS or by automatic extension by extending corporate tax return with IRS

Table 5. (Continued)

Name of routine report (to be provided annually unless noted otherwise)	Agency providing oversight and primary recipient	Plans required to provide report	Applicable laws, regulations, and agency guidance	Form
Annual return/report (5500) schedule MB	Labor, PBGC, and IRS	DB and DC multiemployer plans (DC plans limited to certain money purchase plans)	•26 U.S.C. § 6059. •29 U.S.C. § 1024.	Form 5500 Schedule MB submitted electronically using EFAST2 system. Extension obtained by filing form 5558 with IRS or by automatic extension by extending corporate tax return with IRS
Annual return/report (5500) schedule R—retirement plan information	Labor, PBGC, and IRS	DB and DC large plans (100 or more participants) that have distributed benefits during the plan year	•26 U.S.C. § 6058(a). •29 U.S.C. § 1024.	Form 5500 schedule R submitted electronically using EFAST2 system. Extension obtained by filingform 5558 with IRS or by automatic extension by extending corporate tax return with IRS

Name of routine report (to be provided annually unless noted otherwise)	Agency providing oversight and primary recipient	Plans required to provide report	Applicable laws, regulations, and agency guidance	Form
Annual return/report (5500) schedule SB—plan actuarial information	Labor, PBGC, and IRS	DB single-employer plans	•26 U.S.C. § 6059. •29 U.S.C. § 1024.	Form 5500 schedule SB submitted electronically using EFAST2 system. Extension obtained by filingform 5558 with IRS or by automatic extension by extending corporate tax return with IRS
Annual zone status certification	IRS (must also be provided to plan sponsor)	DB multiemployer plans	•26 U.S.C. § 432(b)(3). •29 U.S.C. § 1085(b)(3).	No form
Premium filings: comprehensive premium filing	PBGC	DB plans (large plans with 500 or more participants provide the reconciliation of the estimated flat rate premium paid earlier in the year with the actual flat rate premium, plans with fewer than 500 participants provide the flat rate premium, and underfunded single-employer plans provide the variable rate premium)	•29 U.S.C. §§ 1306 and 1307. •29 C.F.R. § 4007.3.	Electronic web-based filing using My Plan Administration Account (MyPAA)

Table 5. (Continued)

Name of routine report (to be provided annually unless noted otherwise)	Agency providing oversight and primary recipient	Plans required to provide report	Applicable laws, regulations, and agency guidance	Form
Premium filings: estimated flat-rate premium filing	PBGC	DB large plans (500 or more participants)	•29 U.S.C. §§ 1306 and 1307. •29 C.F.R. § 4007.3.	Electronic web-based filing using My Plan Administration Account (MyPAA)

Source: GAO analysis of information provided by Labor, IRS, and PBGC.

[a] For this table, schedules of the 5500 are counted as separate reports.

Table 6. Plan Sponsors' Routine Disclosures to Participants, Beneficiaries, and Alternate Payees

Name of routine disclosure (to be provided annually unless noted otherwise)	Agency providing oversight and/or guidance	Special instructions about recipients and/or timing of disclosure	Plans required to provide disclosure	Applicable laws, regulations, and agency guidance
Annual funding notice	Labor	In addition to participants, also to be sent to labor organizations representing participants under the plan, each contributing employer in the case of a multiemployer plan, and PBGC	Defined benefit (DB) plans	•29 U.S.C. § 1021(f). •DOL FAB 2009-01 (non-enforcement policy pending further guidance). •Annual Funding Notice for Defined Benefit Plans, 75

Name of routine disclosure (to be provided annually unless noted otherwise)	Agency providing oversight and/or guidance	Special instructions about recipients and/or timing of disclosure	Plans required to provide disclosure	Applicable laws, regulations, and agency guidance
				Fed. Reg. 70.625 (Nov. 18, 2010) (proposed rule) (FAB guidance still in effect until adoption of a final rule). •DOL FAB 2013-01 (non-enforcement policy on additional single-employer plan disclosures required by MAP-21). •Pub. L. No. 112-141, § 40211(b)(2),126 Stat. 405, 848-49 (2012).
Effective opportunity to make or change elective deferrals	IRS		Defined contribution (DC) plans	•26 U.S.C. §§ 401(k)(11)(B)(iii)(II) and 403(b). •26 C.F.R. §§ 1.401(k)-1(e)(2)(ii) and 1.403(b)-5(b)(2).
Eligible automatic contribution arrangement notice (EACA)	IRS		DC plans that have eligible automatic contribution arrangements	•26 U.S.C. § 414(w)(4).

Table 6. (Continued)

Name of routine disclosure (to be provided annually unless noted otherwise)	Agency providing oversight and/or guidance	Special instructions about recipients and/or timing of disclosure	Plans required to provide disclosure	Applicable laws, regulations, and agency guidance
Participant fee disclosures (404(a))	Labor	To be sent annually for plan-related and investment-related; quarterly for administrative and individual expenses actually charged to participants' accounts; on or before the first date a new participant can first direct his or her investments	DC plans administrators of participant-directed individual account plans	•29 C.F.R. § 2550.404a-5 plan-related information may be included in a timely furnished summary plan description under 29 U.S.C. § 1022. •Administrative and individual expenses actually charged to participants' accounts may be included in quarterly benefit statements under 29 U.S.C. § 1025.
Multiemployer pension plan summary plan information	Labor	Rather than to participants, to be sent to contributing employers and employee organizations	DB multiemployer plans (plan administrator)	•29 U.S.C. § 1024(d).

Name of routine disclosure (to be provided annually unless noted otherwise)	Agency providing oversight and/or guidance	Special instructions about recipients and/or timing of disclosure	Plans required to provide disclosure	Applicable laws, regulations, and agency guidance
Notice for fiduciary relief for investments in qualified default investment alternatives (QDIA)	Labor	Initial notice to be provided upon eligibility to participate in the plan, then annually thereafter	DC plans and participant directed DC plans that invest contributions on behalf of participants who fail to give investment direction	•29 U.S.C. § 1104(c)(5). •29 C.F.R. § 2550.404c-5. •(DOL) FAB 2008-3.
Notice of availability of investment advice	Labor		DC plans providing investment advice by asset managers who otherwise receive revenue from the investment of the plan's assets—e.g. a fiduciary advisor	•29 U.S.C. § 1108(g)(6).
Notification to substantial employers	PBGC	Rather than to participants, to be sent to substantial employers	DB single employer plans (plan administrator of plans with at least 2 contributing sponsors not under common control)	•29 U.S.C. § 1366.

Table 6. (Continued)

Name of routine disclosure (to be provided annually unless noted otherwise)	Agency providing oversight and/or guidance	Special instructions about recipients and/or timing of disclosure	Plans required to provide disclosure	Applicable laws, regulations, and agency guidance
Periodic pension benefit statement	Labor	Individual account plans that permit participants and beneficiaries to direct the investment of assets in their account must provide a pension benefit statement at least once each calendar quarter; plans that do not provide participants or beneficiaries a right to direct their investments must provide it at least once each calendar year; and DB plans must provide it at least once every 3 years	DB and DC plans	•29 U.S.C. § 1025. •DOL FAB 2006-3 and 2007-3.
Qualified automatic contribution arrangements (QACA) notice	IRS		DC plans with QACA safe harbor	•26 U.S.C. § 401(k)(12)(D) and (13)(E). •26 C.F.R. § 1.401(k)-3(j).

Name of routine disclosure (to be provided annually unless noted otherwise)	Agency providing oversight and/or guidance	Special instructions about recipients and/or timing of disclosure	Plans required to provide disclosure	Applicable laws, regulations, and agency guidance
Summary annual report (SAR) (contains information from applicable Form 5500)	Labor	In addition to participants, also to be sent to Labor on request	DC and some DB plans (DB plans that are not required to furnish an ERISA § 101(f) (29 U.S.C. § 1021(f)) annual funding notice)	•29 U.S.C. § 1024(b)(3). •29 C.F.R. §§ 2520.104b-10, 2520.104-46(b) and 2520.104b-1.
Summary plan description (SPD)	Labor	In addition to participants, also to be sent to Labor on request. To be sent every 5 years, if SPD was updated; every 10 years, otherwise	DB and DC plans except top hat plans and SEPs that meet the conditions for an alternative method of compliance in 29 C.F.R. §§ 2520.104-23, 2520.104-48 or 2520.104-49. SIMPLEs must comply with disclosure requirements in 29 U.S.C. § 1021	•29 U.S.C. §§ 1022 and 1024(a)(6), (b)(1), (b)(2), (b)(4) and (c). •29 C.F.R. §§ 2520.102-2, 2520.102-3, 2520.104b-1, 2520.104b-2 and 2520.104b-3.

Source: GAO analysis of information provided by Labor, IRS, and PBGC.

Table 7. Plan Sponsors' Nonroutine Reports to Agencies

Name of nonroutine report	Agency providing oversight and primary recipient	Plans required to provide report	Applicable laws, regulations, and agency guidance	Form	Triggering event
Advance notice of reportable events: Application for minimum funding waiver	PBGC	Defined benefit (DB) single-employer plans except public companies or plans with < \$50 million of unfunded vested benefits (UBVs) that are ≥ 90% funded on a vested benefit basis. Waivers may apply to other plans	•29 U.S.C. § 1343. •29 C.F.R. §§ 4043.61 and 4043.66.	Form 10-Advance	Application for minimum fundingwaiver
Advance notice of reportable events: bankruptcy or insolvency	PBGC	DB single-employer plans except public companies or plans with < \$50 million of unfunded vested benefits (UBVs) that are ≥ 90% funded on a vested benefit basis. Waivers may apply to other plans	•29 U.S.C. § 1343. •29 C.F.R. §§ 4043.61 and 4043.68.	Form 10-Advance	Bankruptcy or insolvency

Name of nonroutine report	Agency providing oversight and primary recipient	Plans required to provide report	Applicable laws, regulations, and agency guidance	Form	Triggering event
Advance notice of reportable events: change in contributing sponsor or controlled group	PBGC	DB single-employer plans except public companies or plans with < $50 million of unfunded vested benefits (UBVs) that are ≥ 90% funded on a vested benefit basis. Waivers may apply to other plans	•29 U.S.C. § 1343. •29 C.F.R. §§ 4043.61 and 4043.62.	Form 10-Advance	Change in plan sponsor or controlled group
Advance notice of reportable events: extraordinary dividend or stock redemption	PBGC	DB single-employer plans except public companies or plans with < $50 million of unfunded vested benefits (UBVs) that are ≥ 90% funded on a vested benefit basis. Waivers may apply to other plans	•29 U.S.C. § 1343. •29 C.F.R. §§ 4043.61 and 4043.64.	Form 10-Advance	Extraordinary dividend or stock redemption

Table 7. (Continued)

Name of nonroutine report	Agency providing oversight and primary recipient	Plans required to provide report	Applicable laws, regulations, and agency guidance	Form	Triggering event
Advance notice of reportable events: liquidation	PBGC	DB single-employer plans, except public companies or plans with < \$50 million of unfunded vested benefits (UBVs) that are ≥ 90% funded on a vested benefit basis. Waivers may apply to other plans	•29 U.S.C. § 1343. •29 C.F.R. §§ 4043.61 and 4043.63.	Form 10-Advance	Distress
Advance notice of reportable events: loan default	PBGC	DB single-employer plans except public companies or plans with < \$50 million of unfunded vested benefits (UBVs) that are ≥ 90% funded on a vested benefit basis. Waivers may apply to other plans	•29 U.S.C. § 1343. •29 C.F.R. §§ 4043.61 and 4043.67.	Form 10-Advance	Distress, employer and plan sponsor

Name of nonroutine report	Agency providing oversight and primary recipient	Plans required to provide report	Applicable laws, regulations, and agency guidance	Form	Triggering event
Advance notice of reportable events: transfer of benefit liabilities	PBGC	DB single-employer plans except public companies or plans with < $50 million of unfunded vested benefits (UBVs) that are ≥ 90% funded on a vested benefit basis. Waivers may apply to other plans	•29 U.S.C. § 1343. •29 C.F.R. §§ 4043.61 and 4043.65.	Form 10-Advance	Change in plansponsor
Annual disclosure of financial and actuarial information (4010)	PBGC	DB single-employer plans with one of the following conditions during an information year: funding target attainment percentage (FTAP) <80% for any plan in controlled group OR missed required contributions exceed $1M (statutory lien), OR funding waivers still outstanding, waived amount over $1M	•29 U.S.C. § 1310. •29 C.F.R. pt. 4010.	E-4010 (must be filed electronically using PBGC web-based software at www.pbgc.gov/e4010)	Underfunding

Table 7. (Continued)

Name of nonroutine report	Agency providing oversight and primary recipient	Plans required to provide report	Applicable laws, regulations, and agency guidance	Form	Triggering event
Annual registration statement identifying separated participants with deferred vested benefits (8955-SSA)	IRS (IRS forwards information to SSA)	DB and defined contribution (DC) plans	•26 U.S.C. § 6057(a). •IRS Announcement 2011-21.	IRS form 8955-SSA	Participants who are terminated and not paid out
Application for a waiver of the minimum funding standard (private letter ruling)	IRS (must also be provided to plan participants, beneficiaries, alternate payees, or employee organizations)	DB plans and DC money purchase plans	•26 C.F.R. § 412(c). •Rev. Proc. 2004-15 and other revenue procedures updated annually.	No form	Underfunding

Name of nonroutine report	Agency providing oversight and primary recipient	Plans required to provide report	Applicable laws, regulations, and agency guidance	Form	Triggering event
Application for approval of master or prototype (M&P) or volume submitter defined benefit plan (VSP)	IRS	DB plans	•26 U.S.C. §§ 401(a), 414(j) and 501(a) •Rev Proc. 2011-49	Form 4461 A	Application for approval for M&Por VSP DB Plans
Application for approval of master, prototype, or volume submitter defined contribution plan	IRS	DC plans	•26 U.S.C. §§ 401(a) and 501(a). •Revenue procedures updated annually.	Form 4461 B	Application for approval for M&Por VSP DB Plans
Application for determination for adopters of master, prototype, or volume submitter plans	IRS	DB and DC plans that include a minor modification to the pre-approved volume submitter plan language.	•26 U.S.C. §§ 401(a) and 501(a). •Rev Proc 2007-44. •Other revenue procedures updated annually.	5307	Tax exempt status

Table 7. (Continued)

Name of nonroutine report	Agency providing oversight and primary recipient	Plans required to provide report	Applicable laws, regulations, and agency guidance	Form	Triggering event
Application for determination for employee benefit plan	IRS	DB and DC individually designed plans and any related trusts	•26 U.S.C. §§ 401(a) and 501(a). •Annual Rev. Proc. 20XX-6; 2005-66 and Rev Proc 2007-44. •Other revenue procedures updated annually.	5300	Tax exempt status (Determination letter application for an individuallydesigned plan)
Application for determination for terminating plans	IRS	DB and DC plans, other than multi-employer plans covered by PBGC insurance	•26 U.S.C. § 411(d)(3). •Revenue procedures updated annually.	Forms 5310, 6088, and 8717	Termination
Application for determination of employee stock ownership plan (ESOP)	IRS	DC ESOP plans	•26 U.S.C. §§ 401(a) and 501(a). •Revenue procedures updated annually.	Form 5309 - attachment to Form 5300	Tax exempt status for ESOP plan
Application for extension of time to file certain employee plan returns	IRS	DB and DC plans	•26 U.S.C. § 6081(a). •29 C.F.R. § 1.6081-1(a).	Form 5558	Extension for 5500, 8955-SSA,or 5330

Name of nonroutine report	Agency providing oversight and primary recipient	Plans required to provide report	Applicable laws, regulations, and agency guidance	Form	Triggering event
Application for group trust or pooled trust ruling	IRS	DB and DC (Group or pooled trust sponsors only)	•26 U.S.C. §§ 401(a) and 501(a). •Rev. Rulings 81-1000, 2004-67, and 2011-1. •Other revenue procedures updated annually.	Form 5316	Tax exempt status
Certification of intent to adopt pre-approved plan	IRS	DB and DC plans	•26 U.S.C. §§ 401(a) and 501(a). •Rev. Proc. 2005-66 and 2007-44. •Other revenue procedures updated annually.	Form 8905: Certification of Intent to Adopt Pre-approved Plan. Attachment to Forms 5300, 5307, or 5310	Tax exempt status (adoption of pre-approved plan)
Change in funding method. Private Letter Ruling	IRS	DB plans	•26 U.S.C. § 412(d)(1). •Rev. Proc. 2000-40 and 2000-41. •Other revenue procedures updated annually.	No form	Change in funding

Table 7. (Continued)

Name of nonroutine report	Agency providing oversight and primary recipient	Plans required to provide report	Applicable laws, regulations, and agency guidance	Form	Triggering event
Distributable benefits from employee pension benefit plans	IRS	DB and DC plans	•26 U.S.C. §§ 401(a) and 411(d)(3). •Revenue procedures updated annually.	Form 6088 - attachment to Form 5310 or Form 5300 if collectively bargained termination	Termination with underfunding
Excise taxes related to employee benefit plans	IRS	DB and DC plans	•26 U.S.C. §§ 4971, 4972, 4975, 4978 and 4979A.	Form 5330	Violation of IRC provisions on employee benefitplans
Fiduciary class exemption notice	Labor	DB and DC plans (subject to specified exceptions)	•29 C.F.R. § 2550.408b-2(c)(1)(ix).	Sample available	Service provider fails to provide plan administrator plan level fee disclosure as required by ERISA 408(b)(2) and 29 C.F.R. 2550.408b-2

Name of nonroutine report	Agency providing oversight and primary recipient	Plans required to provide report	Applicable laws, regulations, and agency guidance	Form	Triggering event
Notice of benefit suspension for terminated and insolvent plans	PBGC (must also be provided to participants and beneficiaries)	DB multiemployer plans	•29 U.S.C. § 1441(d)(3). •29 C.F.R. § 4281.32.	No form	Insolvency of terminated plans
Notice of insolvency and annual update: terminated plan	PBGC (must also be provided to participants and beneficiaries)	DB multiemployer plans	•29 C.F.R. §§ 4281.43 and 4281.44.	No form	Insolvency of terminated plans
Notice of insolvency benefit level for terminated plans	PBGC (must also be provided to participants and beneficiaries expected to be in pay status during each insolvency plan year)	DB multiemployer plans	•29 C.F.R. §§ 4281.45 and 4281.46.	No form	Insolvency of terminated plans
Notice of insolvency: reorganization	PBGC (must also be provided to IRS, employers, employee organizations, participants, and beneficiaries	DB multiemployer plans	•29 U.S.C. § 1426(e)(I). •29 C.F.R. § 4245.3.	No form	Insolvency of plan in reorganization (without termination)

Table 7. (Continued)

Name of nonroutine report	Agency providing oversight and primary recipient	Plans required to provide report	Applicable laws, regulations, and agency guidance	Form	Triggering event
Notice of mass withdrawal to PBGC and certifications	PBGC	DB multiemployer plans	•29 C.F.R. §§ 4041A.11, 4219.11(b)(5), 4219.17(c) and (g), and 4219.18(g).	No form	Change in employer (withdrawal of all or substantially all employers) (Not necessary if notice of termination was sent, 29 C.F.R. §4219.17(f))
Notice of merger	PBGC	DB multiemployer plans	•29 U.S.C. § 1411(b)(1). •29 C.F.R. § 4231.8.	No form	Merger (combining assets and liabilities into oneplan) of two or more plans
Notice of merger, consolidation, spinoff, or transfer of plan assets or liabilities to another plan	IRS	DB and DC plans (except multi-employer plans covered by PBGC insurance)	•26 U.S.C. § 6058(b). •Revenue procedures updated annually.	form 5310-A	Change in plan sponsor (merger,consolidati on, spinoff or asset transfer)

Name of nonroutine report	Agency providing oversight and primary recipient	Plans required to provide report	Applicable laws, regulations, and agency guidance	Form	Triggering event
Notice of qualified separate lines of business (QSLOB)	IRS	DB and DC plans	•26 U.S.C. § 414(r). •Revenue procedures updated annually.	Form 5310-A	Elects to be treated as QSLOB
Notification of resource benefit level	PBGC (must also be provided to IRS, employers, employee organizations, participants, and beneficiaries)	DB multiemployer plans	•29 U.S.C. § 1426(e)(2). •29 C.F.R. § 4245.5.	No form	Insolvency of plan in reorganization (without termination)
Notice of substantial cessation of operations	PBGC	DB single-employer plans	•29 U.S.C. §§ 1362(e) and 1363(a).	No form	Change in employer (20 % reduction in active participants resulting from cessations of operations)
Notice of termination	PBGC	DB multiemployer plans	•29 C.F.R. §§ 4041A.11 and 4041A.12.	No form	Termination

Table 7. (Continued)

Name of nonroutine report	Agency providing oversight and primary recipient	Plans required to provide report	Applicable laws, regulations, and agency guidance	Form	Triggering event
Notification of failure to make contribution to a single-employer plan	PBGC	DB single-employer plans	•29 U.S.C. § 1083(k)(4)(A). •29 C.F.R. § 4043.81.	Form 200	Underfunding (unpaid pension payments, including interest,that exceed $1 million)
Plan termination/distress termination: enrolled actuary certification	PBGC	DB single-employer plans	•29 U.S.C. § 1341(c)(2). •29 C.F.R. § 4041.45s.	No form	Termination (distress)
Plan termination/distress termination: notice of request to bankruptcy court to approve distress termination	PBGC	DB single-employer plans	•29 U.S.C. § 1341(c)(2)(B)(ii). •29 C.F.R. § 4041.41(c)(2)(iii).	No form	Termination (distress)

Name of nonroutine report	Agency providing oversight and primary recipient	Plans required to provide report	Applicable laws, regulations, and agency guidance	Form	Triggering event
Plan termination/distress termination: post-distribution certification and missing participant information	PBGC	DB single-employer plans	•29 U.S.C. § 1341(c)(3)(B). •29 C.F.R. § 4041.48.	PBGC 602 and schedule MP (if plan has missing participants)	Termination (distress)
Plan termination/standard termination: termination notice	PBGC	DB single-employer plans	•29 U.S.C. § 1341(b)(2)(A). •29 C.F.R. § 4041.25.	form 500, schedules EA-S and REP-S if designating a representative	Termination (standard)
Post-distribution certification for standard terminations and missing participant information	PBGC	DB single-employer plans	•29 U.S.C. § 1341(b)(3)(A) and (B). •29 C.F.R. §§ 4041.29 and 4050.6(a).	Form 501 & Schedule MP	Termination (standard)

Table 7. (Continued)

Name of nonroutine report	Agency providing oversight and primary recipient	Plans required to provide report	Applicable laws, regulations, and agency guidance	Form	Triggering event
Post-event notice of reportable events: active participant reduction	PBGC	DB single-employer plans	•29 U.S.C. § 1343. •29 C.F.R. §§ 4043.20 and 4043.23.	Form 10-Post-event notification	Active participantreduction
Post-event notice of reportable events: application for minimum funding waiver	PBGC	DB single-employer plans	•29 U.S.C. § 1343. •29 C.F.R. §§ 4043.20 and 4043.33.	Form 10-Post-event notification	Underfunding (application for minimum funding)
Post-event notice of reportable events: bankruptcy or insolvency	PBGC	DB single-employer plans	•29 U.S.C. § 1343. •29 C.F.R. §§ 4043.20 and 4043.35.	Form 10-Post-event notification	Bankruptcy or insolvency

Name of nonroutine report	Agency providing oversight and primary recipient	Plans required to provide report	Applicable laws, regulations, and agency guidance	Form	Triggering event
Post-event notice of reportable events: change in contributing sponsor or controlled group	PBGC	DB single-employer plans	•29 U.S.C. § 1343. •29 C.F.R. §§ 4043.20 and 4043.29.	Form 10-Post-event notification	Change in plan sponsor or controlled group
Post-event notice of reportable events: declaration of extraordinary dividend or stock redemption	PBGC	DB single-employer plans	•29 U.S.C. § 1343. •29 C.F.R. §§ 4043.20 and 4043.31.	Form 10-Post-event notification	Employer redemption of dividend or stock

Table 7. (Continued)

Name of nonroutine report	Agency providing oversight and primary recipient	Plans required to provide report	Applicable laws, regulations, and agency guidance	Form	Triggering event
Post-event notice of reportable events: distribution of $10,000 or more to a substantial owner, causing plan to have unfunded vested benefits	PBGC	DB single-employer plans	•29 U.S.C. § 1343. •29 C.F.R. §§ 4043.20 and 4043.27.	Form 10-Post-event notification	Underfunding[a]
Post-event notice of reportable events: failure to make required minimum funding payment by due date.	PBGC	DB single-employer plans	•29 U.S.C. § 1343. •29 C.F.R. §§ 4043.20 and 4043.25.	Form 10-Post-event notification	Underfunding

Name of nonroutine report	Agency providing oversight and primary recipient	Plans required to provide report	Applicable laws, regulations, and agency guidance	Form	Triggering event
Post-event notice of reportable events: inability of plan to pay benefits when due	PBGC	DB single-employer plans	•29 U.S.C. § 1343. •29 C.F.R. §§ 4043.20 and 4043.26.	Form 10-Post-event notification	Underfunding
Post-event notice of reportable events: liquidation	PBGC	DB single-employer plans	•29 U.S.C. § 1343. •29 C.F.R. §§ 4043.20 and 4043.30.	Form 10-Post-event notification	Distress
Post-event notice of reportable events: loan default	PBGC	DB single-employer plans	•29 U.S.C. § 1343. •29 C.F.R. §§ 4043.20 and 4043.34.	Form 10-Post-event notification	Distress
Post-event notice of reportable events: transfer of benefit liabilities	PBGC	DB single-employer plans	•29 U.S.C. § 1343. •29 C.F.R. §§ 4043.20 and 4043.32.	Form 10-Post-event notification	Change in plan sponsor

Table 7. (Continued)

Name of nonroutine report	Agency providing oversight and primary recipient	Plans required to provide report	Applicable laws, regulations, and agency guidance	Form	Triggering event
Report of withdrawal of substantial employer	PBGC	DB single-employer plans	•29 U.S.C. § 1363(a).	No form[b]	Change in employer (withdrawal of all or substantially all employers). (Specifically, an employer who is a contributing sponsor has ceased operations at a facility with a resulting separation from employment of more than 20% of the participants in the plan or a substantial employer has withdrawn from amultiple employer plan.)

Name of nonroutine report	Agency providing oversight and primary recipient	Plans required to provide report	Applicable laws, regulations, and agency guidance	Form	Triggering event
Request for change in plan/trust year	IRS	DB and DC plans	•26 U.S.C. § 412(d)(1). •Revenue procedures updated annually.	Form 5308	Change in schedule (request change in plan year)
Termination premium declaration	PBGC	DB single-employer plans	•29 U.S.C. § 1306(a)(7). •29 C.F.R. §§ 4006.7 and 4007.13.	Form T	Termination
Top hat statement filing (Top hat plans are certain plans for select group of management or highly compensated employees)	Labor	DC top hat plans	•29 C.F.R. § 2520.104-23.	Content requirements found at 29 § C.F.R. 2520.104-23	Initiation of a tophat plan

Table 7. (Continued)

Name of nonroutine report	Agency providing oversight and primary recipient	Plans required to provide report	Applicable laws, regulations, and agency guidance	Form	Triggering event
User fee for employee plan determination letter request	IRS	DB and DC plans	•26 U.S.C. § 7528. •Rev. Proc. 2005-66 and 2007-44 •Other revenue procedures updated annually.	8717: This form is an attachment to forms 5300, 5307, 5310 and 5316	Tax exempt status

Source: GAO analysis of information provided by Labor, IRS, and PBGC.

[a] Post-event notice of reportable events: distribution of $10,000 or more to a substantial owner, causing plan to have unfunded vested benefits. Under a recent proposed rule, the criteria for a triggering event would be revised to include either distributions to one substantial owner that exceed one percent or to all substantial owners that exceed five percent of plan assets. 78 Fed. Reg. 20,039, 20,063 (Apr. 3, 2013).

[b] Report of withdrawal of substantial employer. There is no form currently, but a proposed regulation includes a form 4062-E for this purpose. 75 Fed. Reg. 48,283, 48,290 (Aug. 10, 2010).

Table 8. Plan Sponsors' Nonroutine Disclosures to Participants, Beneficiaries, and Alternate Payees

Name of nonroutine disclosure	Agency providing oversight and/or guidance	Special instructions about recipients of disclosure	Plans required to provide disclosure	Applicable laws, regulations, and agency guidance	Triggering event
Automatic rollover notice	IRS and Labor		Defined benefit (DB) and defined contribution) DC plans	•26 U.S.C. § 401(a)(31)(B). •29 C.F.R. § 2550.404a-2 (safe harbor for participant disclosures in connection with automatic rollover notice).	Mandatory distribution
Distribution eligible for rollover treatment notice (402(f))	IRS		DB and DC plans	•2 U.S.C. § 402(c) and (f). •26 C.F.R. §§ 1.401(a)-21, 1.402(f)-1 and 1.408-6. •IRS Notices 2009-68 and 2010-84.	Eligible rollover distribution
Distributions from pensions, annuities, retirement or profit sharing plans, IRAs, insurance contracts, etc.	IRS		DB and DC plans	•26 U.S.C. § 6047(d). •26 C.F.R. § 31.3405(c)-1.	Participant takesdistribution

Table 8. (Continued)

Name of nonroutine disclosure	Agency providing oversight and/or guidance	Special instructions about recipients of disclosure	Plans required to provide disclosure	Applicable laws, regulations, and agency guidance	Triggering event
Election to remain under prior vesting schedule	IRS		DB and DC plans	•26 U.S.C. § 411(d)(10).	Change in vesting schedule
Employer stock diversification notice	IRS		DC plans that hold publicly-traded employer securities other than “freestanding” ESOPs with no 401(k) or 401(m) contributions	•26 U.S.C. § 401(a)(35). •29 U.S.C. §§ 1021(m) and 1054 (j). •IRS Notice 2006-107.	Diversification eligibility
ERISA 404(c) disclosure for fiduciary relief	Labor		DC plans. (Disclosure is sent by fiduciaries of participant-directed individual account plans to obtain fiduciary relief related to participants’ investment choices)	•29 U.S.C. § 1104(c). •29 C.F.R. §§ 2550.404c-1 and 2550.404a-5.	Specific plan design

Name of nonroutine disclosure	Agency providing oversight and/or guidance	Special instructions about recipients of disclosure	Plans required to provide disclosure	Applicable laws, regulations, and agency guidance	Triggering event
Extension of amortization period	IRS	In addition to participants, also to be sent to PBGC, contributing employers, and unions	DB multiemployer plans	•26 U.S.C. § 431(d). •29 U.S.C. § 1301(a)(21).	Application for extension
Investments: prospectuses	SEC, FINRA, and Labor		DC plans claiming 404(c) protection or allowing participant investment in employer stock	•15 U.S.C. §§ 77j and 80a-24. •29 C.F.R. § 2550.404a-5(d).	Upon request
Loans: amortization schedule	IRS		DC plans	•26 U.S.C. § 72(p).	Participant requests loan
Multiemployer plan information	Labor	In addition to participants, also to be sent to employee representative or employer obligated to contribute to the plan	DB Multiemployer plans	•29 U.S.C. § 1021(k). •29 C.F.R. § 2520.101-6.	Upon request

Table 8. (Continued)

Name of nonroutine disclosure	Agency providing oversight and/or guidance	Special instructions about recipients of disclosure	Plans required to provide disclosure	Applicable laws, regulations, and agency guidance	Triggering event
Notice of endangered or critical status plans	IRS	In addition to participants, also to be sent to bargaining parties, PBGC, and Labor	DB multiemployer plans	•26 U.S.C. § 432(b)(3). •29 U.S.C. § 1085(b)(3).	Endangered or critical status inplan year
Notice of failure to meet minimum funding standards	Labor	In addition to participants, also to be sent to IRS and PBGC	DB single-employer plans and DC money purchase plans	•29 U.S.C. §§ 1021(d) and 1132(c)(3).	Underfunding (failure to make missed payment within correction period)
Notice of intent to terminate the plan	IRS		DB and DC plans	•26 C.F.R. § 1.7476-2. •Revenue procedures updated annually.	Termination
Notice of mass withdrawal to employers	PBGC		DB multiemployer plans	•29 C.F.R §§ 4219.11(b)(1), 4219.16(a) and 4219.18(d).	Change in employer (withdrawal of allor substantially all employers)

Name of nonroutine disclosure	Agency providing oversight and/or guidance	Special instructions about recipients of disclosure	Plans required to provide disclosure	Applicable laws, regulations, and agency guidance	Triggering event
Notice of participant consent to the distribution	IRS		DC plans	•26 U.S.C. § 411(a)(11). •26 C.F.R. §§ 1.401(a)-20 and 1.411(a)-11(c).	Distribution amount exceeds mandatory cashout limit
Notice of plan termination	Labor		DC individual account plans wanting safe harbor relief	•29 U.S.C. § 1104(a). •29 C.F.R. § 2550.404a-3.	Termination
Notice of qualified change in investment options (QCIO)	Labor	In addition to participants, also to be sent to IRS and PBGC	DC plans	•29 U.S.C. § 1104(c)(4).	Change in plan structure
Notice of qualified domestic relations order (QDRO) procedures	IRS and Labor	Only to be sent to participants, beneficiaries, and alternate payees named in a domestic relations order	DB and DC plans	•26 U.S.C. § 414(p)(6). •29 U.S.C. § 1056(d)(3)(G) (requires a plan to establish procedures in writing).	Marital dissolutions or actions for child or family support

Table 8. (Continued)

Name of nonroutine disclosure	Agency providing oversight and/or guidance	Special instructions about recipients of disclosure	Plans required to provide disclosure	Applicable laws, regulations, and agency guidance	Triggering event
Notice of reallocation liability following mass withdrawal	PBGC	Rather than to participants, to be sent to employers	DB multiemployer plans	•29 C.F.R. § 4219.16(c).	Employer mass withdrawal
Notice of redetermination liability following mass withdrawal	PBGC	Rather than to participants, to be sent to employers liable for redetermination liability	DB multiemployer plans	•29 C.F.R. §§ 4219.16(b) and 4219.18(e).	Employer mass withdrawal
Notice of Reduction in Adjustable Benefits	IRS	In addition to participants, also to be sent to unions and contributing employers	DB multiemployer plans that are critical status	•26 U.S.C. § 432(e)(8)(C).	Critical status
Notice of reorganization	PBGC	Rather than to participants, to be sent to employers and employee organizations	DB multiemployer plans	•29 U.S.C. § 1422.	Change in plan (Reorganization)

Name of nonroutine disclosure	Agency providing oversight and/or guidance	Special instructions about recipients of disclosure	Plans required to provide disclosure	Applicable laws, regulations, and agency guidance	Triggering event
Notice of request for a waiver from minimum funding requirement	IRS		DB target benefit or money purchase plans	•26 U.S.C. § 412(c)(6). •29 U.S.C. § 1082(c)(6).	Underfunding
Notice of restriction on benefit accruals and distributions	IRS and Labor		DB Single-employer plans	•29 U.S.C. §§ 1021(j) and 1132(c)(4).	Underfunding
Notice of right to defer distribution	IRS		DB and DC plans	•26 U.S.C. § 411(a)(11). •Notice To Participants of Consequences of Failing to Defer Receipt of Qualified Retirement Plan Distributions; Expansion of Applicable Election Period and Period for Notices, 73 Fed. Reg. 59,575 (Oct. 9, 2008) (proposed rule and notice of public hearing)[a].	Distribution eligibility

Table 8. (Continued)

Name of nonroutine disclosure	Agency providing oversight and/or guidance	Special instructions about recipients of disclosure	Plans required to provide disclosure	Applicable laws, regulations, and agency guidance	Triggering event
Notice of right to elect not to have federal income tax withheld from distributions	IRS		DB and DC plans	•26 U.S.C. § 3405(e)(10).	Distribution eligibility
Notice of safe harbor discontinuance	IRS		DC safe harbor plans	•26 U.S.C. § 401(k)(12) and(13). •26 C.F.R. § 1.401(k)-3(g).	Discontinuance of safe harbor 401(k) contributions
Notice of significant reduction in the rate of future benefit accruals	IRS	In addition to participants, also to be sent to contributing employer and certain employee organizations	DB and DC plans subject to U.S.C. § 412	•26 U.S.C. § 4980F(e). •29 U.S.C. § 1054(h). •26 C.F.R. § 54.4980F-1.	Amendment of significant reduction in future benefit accrual
Notice of suspension of benefit upon reemployment of retiree	IRS and Labor		DB plans	•26 U.S.C. § 411(a)(3)(B). •29 U.S.C. § 1053(a)(3)(B). •29 C.F.R. § 2530.203-3(b)(4).	Reemployed after retirement

Name of nonroutine disclosure	Agency providing oversight and/or guidance	Special instructions about recipients of disclosure	Plans required to provide disclosure	Applicable laws, regulations, and agency guidance	Triggering event
Notice of transfer of excess pension assets to retiree health benefit account	Labor and IRS	Two-fold notice requirements: one notice to be sent to plan participants and beneficiaries; and a slightly different notice to be sent to Labor, Treasury. and each employee organization representing participants in the plan	DB single-employer plans	•26 U.S.C. §§ 401(h) and 420. •29 U.S.C. § 1021(e). •Minimum Cost Requirement Permitting the Transfer of Excess Assets of a Defined Benefit Pension Plan to a Retiree Health Account, 66 Fed. Reg. 32,897 (June 19, 2001), and (final rule). •DOL Tech Rel. 91-1.	Plan sponsor decision to transfer excess pension assets to a retiree health benefits account
Notice to interested parties of application for advanced determination regarding the qualifications of a plan under Internal Revenue Code	IRS		DB and DC plans filing for 5300, 5307 or 6406 determination letters	•26 C.F.R. §§ 1.7476-1(b), 1.7476-2(e)(1), and 601.201(o)(3)(xiv)-(xx). •Revenue procedures updated annually.	Tax exempt status

Table 8. (Continued)

Name of nonroutine disclosure	Agency providing oversight and/or guidance	Special instructions about recipients of disclosure	Plans required to provide disclosure	Applicable laws, regulations, and agency guidance	Triggering event
Notification of adverse benefit determination	Labor		DB and DC plans	•29 U.S.C. § 1133. •29 C.F.R. § 2560.503-1(f).	Claim for pension benefitsdenied
Participant loan program disclosures	Labor		DB and DC plans	•29 U.S.C. § 1108(b)(1). •26 U.S.C. § 4975(d)(1). •29 C.F.R. § 2550.408b-1.	Participant requests loan
Plan documents (e.g., plan documents, bargaining agreements, trust documents, contracts)	Labor		DB and DC plans	•29 U.S.C. §§ 1024(b)(2) and (b)(4), and 1132(c)(1).	Upon request
Plan termination/distress termination: disclosure of plan termination information	PBGC	In addition to participants, also to be sent to PBGC	DB single-employer plans	•29 U.S.C. § 1341(c)(2)(D). •29 C.F.R. § 4041.51.	Termination (distress)
Plan termination/distress termination: notice of annuity information	PBGC	In addition to participants, also to be sent to PBGC	DB single-employer plans	•29 C.F.R. § 4041.48(c).	Termination (distress)

Name of nonroutine disclosure	Agency providing oversight and/or guidance	Special instructions about recipients of disclosure	Plans required to provide disclosure	Applicable laws, regulations, and agency guidance	Triggering event
Plan termination/distress termination: notice of benefit distribution	PBGC		DB single-employer plans	•29 U.S.C. § 1341(c). •29 C.F.R. § 4041.48(a).	Termination (distress)
Plan terminations/distress termination: notice of intent to terminate (NOIT)	PBGC		DB single-employer plans	•29 U.S.C. § 1341(a)(2). •29 C.F.R. § 4041.43.	Termination (distress)
Plan terminations/standard termination: notice of annuity contract	PBGC		DB single-employer plans	•29 C.F.R. § 4041.28(d).	Termination (standard)
Plan terminations/standard termination: notice of annuity information	PBGC		DB single-employer plans	•29 C.F.R. §§ 4041.23(b)(5) and 4041.27.	Termination (standard)
Plan terminations/standard termination: notice of Intent to Terminate (NOIT)	PBGC		DB single-employer plans	•29 U.S.C. § 1341(a)(2). •29 C.F.R. § 4041.23.	Termination (standard)

Table 8. (Continued)

Name of nonroutine disclosure	Agency providing oversight and/or guidance	Special instructions about recipients of disclosure	Plans required to provide disclosure	Applicable laws, regulations, and agency guidance	Triggering event
Plan terminations/standard termination: notice of plan benefits (NOPB)	PBGC		DB single-employer plans	•29 C.F.R. § 4041.24.	Termination (standard)
Qualified joint and survivor annuity (QJSA) notice	IRS		DB and DC plans subject to 26 U.S.C. § 412	•26 U.S.C. §§ 401(a)(11) and 417(a)(3)(A). •26 C.F.R. § 1.417(a)(3)-1.	Eligibility for benefit payment
Qualified pre-retirement survivor annuity (QPSA) notice	IRS	Only to be sent to married participants age 32-35	DB and DC plans subject to 29 U.S.C. § 412	•26 C.F.R. §§ 401(a)(11)(A) and 417(a)(3)(B). •26 C.F.R. §§ 1.401(a)-20 (Q&A 35) and 1.417(a)(3)-1.	Married participants age32-35
Request for approval of retroactive plan amendment that would reduce accrued benefits	IRS	In addition to participants, also to be sent to employee organizations, and IRS	DB plans	•26 U.S.C. §§ 411(d)(6), 412(d)(2), and 4980F. •29 U.S.C. § 1082(e). •Rev. Proc. 94-42.	Change in plan structure

Name of nonroutine disclosure	Agency providing oversight and/or guidance	Special instructions about recipients of disclosure	Plans required to provide disclosure	Applicable laws, regulations, and agency guidance	Triggering event
Safe harbor 401(k) notice	IRS	In addition to participants, also to be sent to Labor	DC safe harbor plans	•26 U.S.C. § 401(k)(12)(D). •26 C.F.R. §§ 1.401(k)-3(d) and 1.401(k)-3(f).	Change in plan design (safe harbor)
Salary deferral election form	IRS		DC plans with cash or deferral arrangements (CODA)	•26 C.F.R. § 1.401(k)-1(a)(3).	Enrollment
Sarbanes-Oxley blackout notice	Labor		DC plans	•29 U.S.C. § 1021(i). •29 C.F.R. § 2520.101-3(b).	Blackout period
Separated participants with deferred vested benefits	IRS		DB and DC plans	•26 U.S.C. § 6057(e). •29 U.S.C. § 1025(c). •26 C.F.R. § 301.6057-1.	Participants whoare terminated and not paid out that must be reported on Form 8955-SSA

Table 8. (Continued)

Name of nonroutine disclosure	Agency providing oversight and/or guidance	Special instructions about recipients of disclosure	Plans required to provide disclosure	Applicable laws, regulations, and agency guidance	Triggering event
Statement of accrued and nonforfeitable benefits	Labor		DB and DC plans	•29 U.S.C. § 1059.	Upon request, no more than once a year, termination of service, or a oneyear break in service
Summary of material modifications (SMM)	Labor	Labor, upon request	DB and DC plans	•29 U.S.C. §§ 1022 and 1024. •29 C.F.R. § 2520.1-4b-3.	Material modification to the plan

Source: GAO analysis of information provided by Labor, IRS, and PBGC.

[a] Notice of right to defer distribution: the scheduled public hearing was canceled when no one requested to speak. 74 Fed. Reg. 7,021 (Oct. 9, 2008).

APPENDIX III: DISCLOSURES WITH READABILITY PROVISIONS UNDER ERISA OR IRC

Disclosure	Standard	Citation
Annual funding notice	"…shall be written in a manner so as to be understood by the average plan participant."	Labor: 29 U.S.C. § 1021(f)(4)(B).
Eligible automatic contribution arrangement	"…written in a manner calculated to be understood by the average employee to whom the arrangement applies."	IRS: 26 U.S.C. § 414(w)(4)(A)(ii).
Employer stock diversification notice	"The notice required by this subsection shall be written in a manner calculated to be understood by the average plan participant…"	Labor: 29 U.S.C. § 1021(m).
Notice for fiduciary relief for investments in qualified default investment alternatives (QDIA)	"…is written in a manner calculated to be understood by the average employee eligible to participate."	Labor: 29 U.S.C. § 1104(c)(5)(B)(ii).
Notice of availability of investment advice	"…calculated to be understood by the average plan participant…"	IRS: 26 U.S.C. § 4975(f)(8)(H)(i). Labor: 29 U.S.C. § 1108(g)(8)(A).
Notice of reduction in adjustable benefits	"…shall be written in a manner so as to be understood by the average plan participant…"	IRS: 26 U.S.C. § 432(e)(8)(C)(iii)(II). Labor: 29 U.S. C. § 1085(e)(8)(C)(iii)(II).
Notice of significant reduction in the rate of future benefit accruals	"…written in a manner calculated to be understood by the average plan participant…"	IRS: 26 U.S.C. § 4980F(e)(2). Labor: 29 U.S.C. § 1054(h)(2).

Appendix III. (Continued)

Disclosure	Standard	Citation
Periodic pension benefit statement	"…shall be written in a manner calculated to be understood by the average plan participant…"	Labor: 29 U.S.C. § 1025(a)(2)(A)(iii). Labor: 29 U.S.C. § 1025(a)(2)(B)(ii)(II).
Qualified automatic contribution arrangement	"…is written in a manner calculated to be understood by the average employee to whom the arrangement applies…"	IRS: 26 U.S.C. § 401(k)(13)(E)(i)(II).
Sarbanes-Oxley blackout notice	"…shall be written in a manner calculated to be understood by the average plan participant…"	Labor: 29 U.S.C. § 1021(i).
Summary plan description	"…shall be written in a manner calculated to be understood by the average plan participant."	Labor: 29 U.S.C. §§ 1022(a).

Source: Federal laws, as cited above.

End Notes

[1] Pub. L. No. 93-406, 88 Stat. 829 (codified as amended at 26 U.S.C. §§ 401-436 and 4971-4982 and 29 U.S.C. §§ 1001-1453).

[2] Plan sponsors are generally responsible for ensuring that their plans comply with all legal requirements. They may meet such requirements themselves or employ or contract with third parties to meet them. For ease of reference, throughout this report, we use the term "plan sponsor" broadly to include plan administrators, fiduciaries, or other service providers that may provide reports and disclosures on behalf of a plan sponsor.

[3] Throughout this report, we use the term "reports" to refer to the information that plan sponsors are required to provide to federal agencies and the term "disclosures" to refer to the information sponsors are required to provide to participants (including beneficiaries and alternate payees). However, the use of terms regarding reports and disclosures can be confusing. Some reports to agencies include "disclosure" or "notice" in their titles, while some disclosures to participants include "report" or "notice" in their titles. We used those titles when discussing specific reports and disclosures. We also included certain content sent by multiemployer plan sponsors to employers with covered workers as "disclosures."

[4] Model notices are templates created by Labor, PBGC, or IRS for plan sponsors to follow when writing all or a portion of a disclosure.

[5] We assessed the reliability of this call data as well as data from federal agencies on the number of reports they received from plan sponsors in the most recent data year available. We found the data reliable for the purposes of this report.

[6] Pub. L. No. 109-280, 120 Stat. 780.

[7] Another category of plans is multiple employer plans. As with multiemployer plans, multiple employer plans cover employees of more than one employer and can be either DB or DC plans. They differ from multiemployer plans in that no collective bargaining agreements are involved. GAO, *Private Sector Pensions: Federal Agencies Should Collect Data and Coordinate Oversight of Multiple Employer Plans*, GAO-12-665 (Washington D.C.: Sept. 13, 2012).

[8] Certain reports and disclosures define large plans as those with 500 or more participants.

[9] Labor has the statutory authority to bring legal action against plan fiduciaries that do not comply with ERISA requirements. For example, Labor is authorized to assess civil penalties not to exceed $1,000 per day for violations of certain ERISA disclosure requirements. 29 U.S.C. § 1132(c)(4). On January 2, 2009, Labor published final regulations on civil penalties under this authority. Civil Penalties Under ERISA Section 502(c)(4), 74 Fed. Reg. 17.

[10] 26 U.S.C. §§ 162(a)(1) and 404(a).

[11] PBGC insured about 25,500 DB plans protecting some 43 million workers and retirees in 2012. PBGC covers most DB plans, but not all. DB plans not covered by PBGC include plans for professional service employees (such as doctors and lawyers) with fewer than 26 employees, church plans, and public plans provided to federal, state, and local government workers. 29 U.S.C. § 1341.

[12] In addition, publicly-traded companies must include in their annual financial statements, also filed with the SEC, financial information on their pension plans just as they do on other company financial matters. With respect to annual reports, the plan sponsor is treated essentially as any other such offerer of stock, and with respect to financial statements, plan information is included basically to present a more complete picture of a company's financial situation. Since, for the most part, companies can meet SEC pension plan reporting

requirements by simply providing copies of their plan's financial statements, we did not include these SEC reporting requirements in the scope of this report.

[13] Pub. L. No. 104-13, sec. 2, § 3504(c)(1),109 Stat. 163, 167.

[14] While some of the requirements have been created directly by statute, others have been created by the three agencies in implementing the law.

[15] Pub. L. No. 107-204, § 306(b), 116 Stat. 745, 780-83 (codified at 29 U.S.C. § 1021(i)). The act amended ERISA to add a new requirement that individual account pension plans provide notice to participants and beneficiaries in advance of periods during which the ability of participants or beneficiaries to direct or diversify assets credited to their accounts, to obtain loans from the plan or to obtain distributions from the plan will be temporarily suspended, limited or restricted. Enron was a large energy company that was plagued by financial fraud and insider trading and ultimately went bankrupt. Before the bankruptcy, when the value of Enron stock was plummeting, its rank and file DC plan participants were not permitted to sell their Enron shares and, therefore, suffered greater losses than they may have otherwise. H.R. Rep. 107-414, at 18 (2002).

[16] §§ 501-509, 120 Stat. 936-952.

[17] Fiduciary Requirements for Disclosure in Participant-Directed Individual Account Plans, 75 Fed. Reg. 64,910 (Oct 20, 2010); Reasonable Contract of Arrangement Under Section 408(b)(2)—Fee Disclosure, 75 Fed. Reg. 41,600 (July 16, 2010) and Requirements for Fee Disclosure to Plan Fiduciaries and Participants—Applicability Dates, 76 Fed. Reg. 42,539 (July 19, 2011).

[18] 29 U.S.C. § 1021(a) and (b). Certain plans, such as SIMPLE individual retirement accounts (IRA) are not subject to Form 5500 requirements. The Form 5500 includes 9 schedules and additional attachments that are required depending on the plan's characteristics and circumstances. The schedules and attachments are listed separately in our report. GAO is conducting a related study of the Form 5500 report anticipated to be released in spring, 2014.

[19] Schedule I is not required of plans filing the 5500-SF or 5500 EZ. In plan year 2011, 91,377 plans submitted a schedule H and 111,069 plans submitted a schedule I with additional financial information.

[20] Schedule A is only required of plans with benefits provided by an insurance company. In plan year 2011, 120,263 plans submitted at least one schedule A to report benefits provided by an insurance company.

[21] In plan year 2011, plan sponsors submitted fewer than 900 filings of schedule G to report loans or fixed income obligations in default or classified as uncollectible.

[22] ERISA agencies collect data on the volume of certain reports they receive but are unable to track similar information on disclosures.

[23] 29 U.S.C. § 1024(b).The SPD must be provided to participants within 90 days of becoming a participant or first receiving benefits. If any material changes are made to the plan, a copy of the summary of material modifications must be sent to participants 210 days after the close of the plan year in which the modification took place and an SPD sent every fifth year. If no material changes occurred, a new SPD must be provided every tenth year.

[24] 29 U.S.C. § 1021(f).

[25] 29 U.S.C. § 1025(a).

[26] 29 C.F.R. § 4007.3. Large DB plans with 500 or more participants are required to submit an annual flat-rate premium filing. Plans with 500 or more participants provide reconciliation of the estimated flat-rate premium paid earlier in the year with the actual flat-rate premium,

plans with fewer than 500 participants provide the flat-rate premium, and underfunded single-employer plans provide the variable-rate premium.

[27] Single-employer DB plans submit schedule SB (40,083 submitted in plan year 2011) and multiemployer DB plans and certain money purchase plans submit schedule MB (1,326 submitted in plan year 2011).

[28] 29 U.S.C. § 1024(d).The multiemployer summary plan information is not provided to participants but only to contributing employers and employee organizations.

[29] 29 U.S.C. § 1366. The notification to substantial employers is not provided to participants, but only to contributing sponsors that constitute a substantial employer for the preceding year to notify them of this status.

[30] 26 C.F.R. §§ 1.401(k)-1(e)(2)(ii) and 1.403(b)-5(b)(2).

[31] 29 C.F.R. § 2550.404a-5.

[32] 26 U.S.C. § 401(k)(13). Certain 401(k) plans, including some automatic enrollment plans, use a specific design known as a safe harbor. 26 U.S.C. § 401(k)(12) and 13. Such plans are deemed to satisfy the applicable test to determine that a plan does not discriminate in favor of highly-compensated employees by meeting either the nonelective contribution or matching contribution requirement. They are divided into two types based on their inclusion of additional optional criteria, such as automatic enrollment and the level of contributions. 26 C.F.R. § 1.401(k)-3(a) and (b).

[33] GAO, *Retirement Savings: Automatic Enrollment Shows Promise for Some Workers, but Proposals to Broaden Retirement Savings for Other Workers Could Face Challenges*, GAO-10-31 (Washington, D.C.: Oct. 23, 2009).

[34] 29 U.S.C. § 1104(c)(5).

[35] 26 U.S.C. § 414(w)(4).

[36] 26 U.S.C. § 401(k)(13)(E).

[37] 29 U.S.C. § 1108(g)(6). One survey, conducted by SEI Research, found that 78 percent of DC plans partner with a fiduciary advisor. SEI Defined Contribution Management Research Panel Survey. February 2012. The poll was completed by 138 executives overseeing U.S. DC plans ranging in size from $25 million to over $3 billion in assets.

[38] 26 U.S.C. § 6057(e) and 29 U.S.C § 1025(c). Plan sponsors must also file an 8955-SSA when previously reported participants with deferred vested benefits receive a distribution of those benefits. In plan year 2012, plan sponsors submitted 316,581 8955-SSAs, which is equal to about one-third of the Form 5500, EZ, and SF reports filed in fiscal year 2011.

[39] Agencies provided data from various time periods measured by plan years and fiscal years from 2011-2012.

[40] Specifically, the law requires single-employer DB plans to provide PBGC with information annually regarding the plan's assets and liabilities and copies of the plan's financial statements if any of the plan's contributing sponsors or control group members maintained a plan that meets one of the following conditions during an information year: (1) a plan with a funding target attainment percentage of less than 80 percent; (2) a plan that meets the conditions for imposition of a lien; or (3) a plan that has been granted minimum funding waivers in excess of $1 million and a portion is still outstanding. 29 U.S.C. § 1310. Certain waivers apply if, for example, the controlled group's aggregate underfunding does not exceed $15 million. 29 C.F.R. § 4010.11.

[41] Section 4010 filers file at the corporate (controlled group) level and provide information at the plan level in the same filing. Controlled group submissions may include information for more than one plan. The 340 submissions in 2011 represents 598 plans. Due to the grouped filing and exceptions and waivers regarding who must file a 4010, the number of plans

represented in 4010 submissions is significantly smaller than the number of underfunded plans.

[42] ERISA imposes certain obligations on plan fiduciaries. Under ERISA, a person generally acts as a plan fiduciary when he or she (1) exercises any discretionary control or authority over plan management or any authority or control over plan assets, (2) renders investment advice for compensation respecting plan assets, or has authority or responsibility to do so, or (3) has any discretionary authority or responsibility over plan administration. 29 U.S.C. § 1002(21).

[43] 29 U.S.C. § 1021(f)(1).

[44] 29 U.S.C. § 1426(e)(2).

[45] GAO, *Private Pensions: Timely and Accurate Information Is Needed to Identify and Track Frozen Defined Benefit Plans*, GAO-04-200R (Washington, D.C.: Dec 17, 2003).

[46] *www.dol.gov/ebsa/pdf/rdguide.pdf.*

[47] *http://www.pbgc.gov/prac/reporting-and-disclosure.html.*

[48] *http://www.irs.gov/Retirement-Plans/Plan-Sponsor/A-Plan-Sponsor's-Responsibilities.*

[49] *http://www.irs.gov/Retirement-Plans/Plan-Participant,-Employee/Retirement-Topics—-Notices.*

[50] Exec. Order No. 13,563, 76 Fed. Reg. 3821 (Jan. 21, 2011). This order calls for a periodic review of existing regulations and determination of whether any of them should be modified, streamlined, expanded or repealed.

[51] Amendments to the Abandoned Plan Regulations, 77 Fed. Reg. 74,063 (Dec. 12, 2012).

[52] Reportable Events and Certain Other Notification Requirements, 78 Fed. Reg. 20,039 (Apr. 3, 2013). PBGC has also proposed revisions to premium due dates and related changes intended to reduce regulatory burden. Premium Rates; Payment of Premiums; Reducing Regulatory Burden, 78 Fed. Reg. 44,056 (July 23, 2013)

[53] 44 U.S.C. § 3506(b)(1)(A). A central goal of OMB review is to help agencies strike a balance between collecting information necessary to fulfill their statutory missions and guarding against unnecessary or duplicative information that imposes unjustified costs on the American public. Under the Paperwork Reduction Act, OMB may approve a request for information collection for up to three years at one time. 44 U.S.C. § 3507(g).

[54] 29 C.F.R. § 2550.408b-2. Because such reporting is from service providers to plan sponsors and fiduciaries it is not included in our lists of required reports and disclosures submitted by plan sponsors in appendix II.

[55] 29 U.S.C. § 1024.

[56] We evaluated summaries of calls to Labor benefits advisors from participants and beneficiaries between October 1, 2011 and December 31, 2012, to more fully include the perspective of participants on disclosures in this review. The information is not representative of the views of all plan participants, but only those who called Labor. The information we reviewed took the form of summaries logged by benefits advisors, not full transcripts of conversations.

[57] Form SSA-L99-C1.

[58] 26 U.S.C. § 6057(a). Each month, SSA checks the name and Social Security number of each new claimant for Social Security benefits to determine whether the claimant is listed in SSA's pension benefit record. SSA mails a notice to each new claimant that the data indicates may be entitled to a benefit.

[59] The SSA mails about 90,000 of these notices to new Social Security claimants each month, as required under 42 U.S.C. § 1320b-1(a). SSA also sends these notices to individuals upon request, and to claimants of a lump-sum death payment or hospital insurance coverage under Title XVIII of the Social Security Act. The notice is provided on Form SSA L99-C1.

[60] A recent study by the SSA's Office of Inspector General found that when participants inquired about the benefits listed in the notice, they sometimes found that they were not actually due. Specifically, the study found that of the 14 cases they reviewed where participants made inquiries that had been resolved, 11 were not due benefits. Social Security Administration, Office of the Inspector General, *Quick Response Evaluation, Employee Retirement Income Security Act Notices*, A-13-11-01141, September, 2011.

[61] Data on participant calls to Labor show that Labor also helps participants understand the notice.

[62] The potential private pension benefit information notice (Form SSA-L99-C1) states: "If you have questions, you should contact the Plan Administrator. If you cannot locate the Plan Administrator, contact your former employer. If you cannot locate your former employer, check the reference department of your local library or contact your State's corporation commission. This agency should be in the State Government section of the telephone directory."

[63] Although the data on benefits owed is not verified, SSA officials said they do verify that the Social Security number listed in the notice is valid.

[64] 26 U.S.C. § 6011(e)(1). The information on the 8955-SSA was previously included on the Form 5500. However, when the 5500 was required to be submitted electronically in 2010, the form was stripped of information that was required to be reported to IRS to comply with the statutory prohibition. As a result, a separate 8955-SSA form was created. Treasury recently proposed regulations that would mandate electronic filing for form 8955- SSA to the extent permitted by current statute. Employee Retirement Benefit Plan Returns Required on Magnetic Media, 78 Fed. Reg. 53,704 (Aug. 30, 2013).

[65] We previously reported on the challenges of the 401(k) rollover process (GAO-13-30). If a participant's pool of retirement savings is fragmented across multiple plans and IRAs, over time, the sum of the fees associated with the various plans may be greater than if the participant had consolidated their savings. We previously reported that even a seemingly small fee, such as a 1 percent annual charge, can significantly reduce 401(k) plan savings over the course of an individual's career. GAO, *Private Pensions: Changes Needed to Provide 401(k) Plan Participants and the Department of Labor Better Information on Fees*, GAO-07-21 (Washington, D.C.: Nov. 16, 2006).

[66] In response to a provision in the PPA (§ 410, 120 Stat. 934-35), PBGC recently published a request for information from the public about including the benefits of missing participants in terminating individual account (i.e., DC) plans. Missing Participants in Individual Account Plans, 78 Fed. Reg. 37,598 (June 21, 2013). Under ERISA, PBGC locates missing participants in insured DB single-employer plans that have terminated (29 U.S.C. § 1350), and is currently in the process of expanding the program to include DC plans, multiemployer DB plans, and the plans of small professional services employers.

[67] For more on how we evaluated disclosures on these factors, see appendix 1.

[68] ERISA established an Advisory Council on Employee Welfare and Pension Benefit Plans, known as the ERISA Advisory Council (EAC). 29 U.S.C. § 1142.The duties of the EAC are to advise the Secretary of Labor and submit recommendations regarding the Secretary's functions under ERISA.

[69] The EAC solicited testimony from witnesses from a broad cross-section of the retirement community, including Labor officials and representatives from associations, service providers, academics, and participant advocacy groups in 2009. See Advisory Council on Employee Welfare and Pension Benefit Plans. *Promoting Retirement Literacy and Security*

by Streamlining Disclosures to Participants and Beneficiaries, accessed October 2, 2012, http://www.dol.gov/ebsa/publications/2009ACreport2.html.

[70] Representatives of one participant advocacy group noted that, to help participants better understand their benefits; participants should also have continuous access to previous SPDs, as well as better information about their benefits. Specifically, it was suggested that those in DC plans should be provided projected monthly benefits at different retirement ages (i.e., if their current savings were converted to a lifetime annuity at age 55, 60, and 65). In 2010, Labor and IRS published a request for information that would be relevant to such a suggestion. Request for Information Regarding Lifetime Income Options for Participants and Beneficiaries in Retirement Plans, 75 Fed. Reg. 5,253 (Feb. 2, 2010). Another participant advocate said participants in DB plans should be provided information about how their benefit was calculated (i.e., if the formula is 30 percent of the average of the 3 highest earning years, participants should be provided the data used in the calculation—specifically, which were the highest earning years and how much income was recorded for each of those years).

[71] Labor provides a link to a model notice which satisfies the disclosures required by both the IRC (26 U.S.C. §§ 401(k)(13) and 414(w)), and ERISA (29 U.S.C. §§ 1104(c)(5) and 1144(e)(3)) in Field Assistance Bulletin 2008-03, http://www.irs.gov/pub/irs-tege/sample_notice.pdf.

[72] We previously recommended Congress consider consolidating these funding notices to eliminate duplication. GAO, *Private Pensions: Changes Needed to Better Protect Multiemployer Pension Benefits*, GAO-11-79 (Washington, D.C.: October 18, 2011).

[73] GAO, *Private Pensions: Changes Needed to Better Protect Multiemployer Pension Benefits*, GAO-11-79 (Washington, D.C.: Oct. 18, 2011).

[74] U.S. Department of Labor, Summary Plan Description Requirements under ERISA: Supporting Statement for Paperwork Reduction Act Submissions, OMB Number 1210- 0039, April 2013.

[75] In addition, when the plan administrator changes the content of the SPD, participants are not required to be provided a summary of the material modifications until 210 days after the end of the plan year in which the change was made. In testimony before the EAC in 2005, several witnesses said that deadline was so late it made the summary useless to the participant.

[76] Actuarial information included in the annual report must be displayed on any intranet website maintained by the plan sponsor for the purpose of communicating with employees. 29 U.S.C. § 1024(b). Generally, a plan's full annual report is publicly available online on Labor's website. We also found several employers willing to post their plan's SPD to their public website.

[77] In the past, plan sponsors were also required to file SPDs with Labor. The Taxpayer Relief Act of 1997 eliminated that requirement.

[78] The rollover notice is required under 26 U.S.C. § 402(f). We recently reported that 401(k) plan participants separating from their employers need help to obtain and understand information about their distribution options. If participants have more than $5,000 in their account and are not normal retirement age, they can generally leave their funds with their previous employer, but the 402(f) notice does not mention that option. We reported that an employer-sponsored plan environment generally has lower fees and better comparative information. Also, with employer-sponsored plans, ERISA plan fiduciaries are required to select and monitor investment options in the best interest of participants. GAO, *401(k) Plans: Labor*

and IRS Could Improve the Rollover Process for Participants, GAO-13-30 (Washington, D.C.: March 7, 2013).

[79] A fiduciary shall discharge his duties with respect to a plan solely in the interest of the participants and beneficiaries and for the exclusive purpose of providing benefits to participants and their beneficiaries and defraying reasonable expenses of administering the plan. 29 U.S.C. § 1104.

[80] In some instances, the statute expressly provides that agencies are to treat sponsors as having complied with a particular disclosure requirement if model notices are used. But, because a given model cannot apply in all circumstances, the instructions generally direct the plan sponsor to provide additional content as appropriate for the plan. For example, the instructions for the QACA model notice state that a plan sponsor will need to add to, subtract from, or otherwise change the sample notice to the extent a plan's form and operations differ from the hypothetical QACA described in the sample notice, so that the actual notice accurately reflects the provisions of the plan.

[81] For example, one participant advocacy group testified before the EAC that model notices are a great help to employers, but they are also vitally important to participants because notices generated by plans are often confusing.

[82] Plain Language Action and Information Network, *Federal Plain Language Guidelines*, (March 2011), accessed September 6, 2013, http://www.plainlanguage.gov /howto/guidelines /bigdoc/fullbigdoc.pdf. Federal plain language guidelines are maintained by federal employees. For further details on our plain language analysis, see app. I. The Plain Writing Act of 2010 also calls for writing that is consistent with best practices appropriate for the intended audience. 5 U.S.C. § 301. Such writing avoids jargon, redundancy, ambiguity, and obscurity.

[83] For further details on our methodology for conducting this analysis, see appendix I. None of the agencies provides a comprehensive list of model notices. As a result, we continued to discover additional models over the course of our review. We conducted this readability analysis on the first 10 of the 16 we identified (see table 3). In addition, we identified other instances of agency model language for certain situations. For example, we found sample language on Labor's website to help plan sponsors prepare disclosures dealing with qualified domestic relations orders, and a sample paragraph in Labor's regulations (29 C.F.R. § 2520.102-2) for plan sponsors to use when they need to explain to non-English speakers how to obtain assistance understanding their SPD.

[84] The models we reviewed were all written in English. While none of them contained sample language plan sponsors could use to inform non-English speakers how to obtain assistance in their language, we did find that IRS produced a version of the Saver's Credit model notice in Spanish as well as English in IRS Announcement 2001-120.

[85] 29 C.F.R. §§ 2520.102-2(c) and 1520.104b-10(e). Specifically, assistance must be offered if the plan contains under 100 participants and 25 percent are literate only in the same foreign language, or if the plan covers more than 100 participants and either 500 participants or 10 percent of participants, whichever is less, are literate in only that same foreign language.

[86] To determine the reading level at which model notices were written, we selected and used one of many widely available automated readability tools, the Flesch-Kincaid Grade-Level (FKGL) test. For more on the FKGL tool, see app. I. However, a participant advocacy group representative noted that to gauge understandability, it is important to also take the organization and presentation of the content into account. Another participant advocacy group representative suggested that to ensure understandability model notices should be field-tested with people who have low levels of education.

[87] In contrast, the Social Security Administration standards require its disclosures to be written between a sixth- and eighth-grade reading level.

[88] Labor officials also consider their benefits advisors program, in which benefits advisors are available to field phone calls from participants, as addressing readability. We considered disclosure readability based solely on the written content of disclosures sent to participants. Participants who call Labor and ask a benefits advisor to explain disclosure content may gain a better understanding of the content than participants who do not call.

End Notes for Appendix I

[1] In some instances, the model disclosure provided a template for only a portion of the content a participant would receive. For example, Labor provides a model statement of participant rights under The Employee Retirement Income Security Act of 1974 (ERISA) to be included in the summary plan description (SPD), and a model comparative chart to be included in participant fee disclosures, but the disclosures are required to include additional information beyond the text in the models.

[2] Federal plain language guidelines are maintained by federal employees and are available at www.plainlanguage.gov. Plain Language Action and Information Network, *Federal Plain Language Guidelines*, (March 2011), accessed September 6, 2013,

[3] This part of our readability analysis included the first 10 model disclosures we identified over the course of our review.

End Note for Appendix II

[1] Throughout the report, disclosures to participants include those to beneficiaries and alternate payees. We also identified a small number of disclosures made by multiemployer plan sponsors to employers.

In: Private-Sector Pensions
Editor: Christian Wong

ISBN: 978-1-63482-608-2

Chapter 2

PRIVATE PENSIONS: REVISED ELECTRONIC DISCLOSURE RULES COULD CLARIFY USE AND BETTER PROTECT PARTICIPANT CHOICE*

United States Government Accountability Office

ABBREVIATIONS

DB	defined benefit
DC	defined contribution
ERISA	Employee Retirement Income Security Act of 1974
E-SIGN	Electronic Signatures in Global and National Commerce Act
PPA	Pension Protection Act of 2006
PDF	portable document format

WHY GAO DID THIS STUDY

With the advent of new technology, sponsors of U.S. private-sector pension plans have begun to deliver plan information to participants

* This is an edited, reformatted and augmented version of The United States Government Accountability Office publication, GAO-13-594, dated September 2013.

electronically in an effort to reduce plan costs and provide greater participant choice. Yet there are concerns that use of electronic disclosure could make it more difficult for some plan participants to receive important information about their plans. GAO was asked to review issues related to electronic disclosure. For this report, GAO: (1) examined the extent to which law and regulations permit electronic disclosure to participants; (2) explored the reported advantages and disadvantages associated with electronic delivery; and (3) evaluated the weaknesses identified, if any, in the agencies' electronic delivery requirements. In conducting this work, GAO reviewed and analyzed relevant federal statutes and regulations; stakeholder responses to Labor's 2011 request for information on electronic disclosure; and any weaknesses identified in interviews of participant advocates and industry representatives, selected by GAO to capture a broad array of perspectives.

What GAO Recommends

GAO recommends that Labor and Treasury consider clarifying regulatory requirements and expanding participants' ability to opt out of electronic delivery. In its written comments, Labor generally agreed with the report's findings and recommendations. Treasury and the Pension Benefit Guaranty Corporation did not provide formal written comments. All three agencies provided technical comments.

What GAO Found

Federal statutes and regulations under the purview of the Department of Labor (Labor) and the Department of the Treasury (Treasury) allow employers who sponsor private pension plans to furnish all pension disclosures to participants electronically:

- as the default delivery method if participants meet specific criteria regarding access, or
- if affirmative consent is obtained.

When neither of these conditions can be met, or when requested by participants, plan sponsors must send paper disclosures.

Industry representatives and participant advocates reported various advantages and disadvantages concerning the use of electronic delivery. Both groups agreed that the popularity of electronic delivery was growing due to various efficiencies—such as reduced costs and better tracking of disclosures—that can be advantageous to both pension plan sponsors and participants. However, both groups also raised concerns with the requirements associated with electronic delivery, citing issues with their lack of consistency and clarity as well as concerns that they may not adequately protect a participant's right to opt to receive paper disclosures.

Pros and Cons of Electronic Delivery of Pension Disclosures

	Cost	Access and archiving	Security	Receipt
Pros	No printing and mailing costs for sponsors that could add to indirect costs passed on to participants	Electronic notices are always available and easy to archive	Passwords can help protect personal information	Delivery, and "bounce back" return of undeliverable notices is immediate
Cons	Costs of maintaining computer, Internet connection, and printing incurred by participants	May lose access to notices if computer malfunctions or Internet connection is lost	Vulnerable to security breach from hacking and phishing	Undeliverable notices must be re-sent by mail, no way to know if notice sent to unused account

Source: GAO analysis of Labor dataand interviews with agency officials, industry representatives and participant advocacy groups.

GAO's analysis of these concerns identified several weaknesses in the current electronic delivery requirements. For example, although agencies are to draft regulations that avoid inconsistency across agencies and are easy to understand, GAO found that Labor's and Treasury's requirements describing which participants qualify for default electronic delivery to be somewhat inconsistent and unclear, which may impede use of electronic delivery by some plan sponsors. GAO also found that, although participants may request paper disclosures at any time, requirements permitting default electronic delivery and sponsors' use of a secured website to furnish disclosures may not fully protect a participant's ability to choose paper as their preferred delivery method on an ongoing, rather than a document-by-document, basis.

* * *

September 13, 2013

The Honorable Tom Harkin
Chairman
Committee on Health, Education, Labor and Pensions
United States Senate

The Honorable George Miller
Ranking Member
Committee on Education and the Workforce
House of Representatives

The Employee Retirement Income Security Act of 1974 (ERISA)[1] requires private-sector employers sponsoring pension plans to issue a variety of informational notices to plan participants and beneficiaries, including at enrollment, on a quarterly and annual basis, and when certain events occur, such as job or plan termination. The Department of Labor (Labor) and the Department of the Treasury (Treasury) are responsible for overseeing this disclosure regime, with the purpose of ensuring that participants and beneficiaries have access to plan information to help them make informed decisions about their retirement. Such information is especially important for the tens of millions of participants and beneficiaries who are responsible for making investment decisions regarding contribution levels, asset allocation, and adequacy of savings in their plans.

The proliferation of new forms of electronic devices and communication over the last decade and changes in how some employees access information have changed the way some employers communicate with their employees, leading some private-sector plan sponsors and participants to seek to expand use of electronic media to furnish plan information to participants. In 2011, in response to an executive order[2] and other administration policies encouraging electronic dissemination of information, Labor solicited public views, suggestions, and comments on whether—and possibly how—to expand or modify the department's 2002 electronic disclosure regulations for pension plans to take into account current technology, best practices, and the need to protect the rights and interests of participants and beneficiaries. In its request for information,[3] Labor acknowledged the need to balance the efficiencies of electronic disclosure—lower employer costs and administrative burden, timeliness, and accuracy—with protections for U.S. workers who may not have reasonable access to the Internet or simply prefer to receive traditional paper disclosures.

You asked us to explore several aspects of electronic disclosure. This report: (1) examines the extent to which federal law and regulations permit electronic disclosure to participants; (2) explores the reported advantages and disadvantages associated with the use of electronic delivery of retirement information; and (3) evaluates the weaknesses identified, if any, in the agencies' requirements for use of electronic delivery.

To examine the extent to which federal laws and regulations permit electronic disclosure, we reviewed and analyzed the relevant federal laws, regulations and guidance related to providing plan information to participants electronically; interviewed officials at Labor and Treasury; and consulted relevant literature. Next, we conducted a comparative analysis of the relevant Labor and Treasury regulations governing electronic delivery to determine which disclosures and which participants qualified for electronic delivery. We limited the scope of our analysis to the pension-related disclosures that plan sponsors are required to furnish to participants and did not examine other disclosures required for employee benefit plans such as those applicable to health and welfare programs, those required under the purview of the Pension Benefit Guaranty Corporation, or participant disclosures provided by the agencies. In this report, we use the term "participants" in general reference to all active, retired, and separated vested participants and their beneficiaries (e.g., surviving spouses and alternate payees) who are entitled to disclosures under Title I of ERISA and the Internal Revenue Code.

To explore the reported advantages and disadvantages associated with the use of electronic delivery, we analyzed the 78 written responses from participant advocates and industry representatives to Labor's 2011 request for information on electronic disclosure; reviewed relevant literature; and conducted semi-structured interviews with 21 representatives from 11 participant advocacy groups and with 57 industry representatives (including individuals from 10 service providers, 8 plan sponsor advocacy groups, and 2 large plan sponsors). The interview information gathered was not generalizable beyond the individuals we interviewed. However, to ensure that we gathered input from entities that represented large numbers of plans and participants, we selected service providers ranked among the largest 31 recordkeepers (as ranked in 2011 by *Pensions & Investments*) for assets under management, plan sponsors served, and number of participants, and who served plan sponsors of both large and small pension plans. To select plan sponsors, industry representatives, and participant advocates for interviews, we used an iterative process to identify knowledgeable stakeholders, and selected for interviews those who would provide us with a broad range of perspectives on issues surrounding the electronic disclosure of pension plan and retirement information. At each interview, we solicited names of additional stakeholders it would be useful to interview until we had coverage of a broad range of perspectives on electronic disclosure.

To evaluate any weaknesses in the agencies' requirements for electronic delivery, we examined the laws and regulations related to the concerns raised by industry representatives and participant advocates. Based on this review, we identified ways that the requirements for electronic delivery could be improved to help address their concerns.

We conducted this performance audit from September 2012 to August 2013 in accordance with generally accepted government auditing standards. Those standards require that we plan and perform the audit to obtain sufficient, appropriate evidence to provide a reasonable basis for our findings and conclusions based on our audit objectives. We believe that the evidence obtained provides a reasonable basis for findings and conclusions based on our audit objectives.

BACKGROUND

ERISA requires the disclosure of certain pension plan and investment-related information, including fee and expense information, to participants in private-sector plans. The Internal Revenue Service at Treasury and Employee Benefits Security Administration at Labor are primarily responsible for enforcing laws that govern these plans. Treasury interprets and enforces provisions of the Internal Revenue Code that apply to tax-qualified plans. Labor enforces ERISA reporting and disclosure provisions and fiduciary responsibility standards, which among other things, concern the type and extent of information provided to plan participants.

Types of Plans

Private-sector pension plans are classified either as defined benefit (DB) or as defined contribution (DC) plans.[4] DB plans generally offer a fixed level of monthly retirement income based upon a formula specified in the plan (which often takes into account factors such as years of service and age at retirement), regardless of how the plan's investments perform. In contrast, in DC plans, such as 401(k) plans, benefit levels depend on the contributions made to the plan and the performance of the investments in individual accounts, which may fluctuate in value over time. Over the past 4 decades, DC plans have become the principal retirement savings vehicle for U.S. workers participating in employer-sponsored plans. Unlike employees with more traditional DB pensions, participants in DC plans typically bear responsibility for funding and managing their investments in a way that seeks to achieve sufficient benefits in retirement. The rapid growth in participant-directed DC plans has shifted much of the investment risk and decision-making from the plan sponsor to the participant. In 2010, Labor reported that U.S. employers sponsored 46,543 DB plans with about 41 million participants and 654,469 DC plans with about 88 million participants. As shown in figure 1, there has been a significant growth in the number of small DC plans; however, the majority of participants are in large DC plans.

According to the most recent employee benefits survey by the U.S. Bureau of Labor Statistics, employee participation in employer-sponsored plans remained low in 2012, with 65 percent of private-industry employees having access to plans and 48 percent participating in their employer-sponsored DB or DC plan. In addition, the data show that one in four employees who had access to a plan through their employer did not enroll in their employer's plan. Moreover, the overall enrollment rate for high-wage employees in DC plans was twice the enrollment rate of low-wage employees. In response to concerns that many employees were not participating in the DC plans offered by their employers, the Pension Protection Act of 2006 (PPA) included various incentives for employers to adopt autoenrollment.[5] Under autoenrollment, plan sponsors enroll employees automatically into their DC plans, unless employees explicitly choose not to participate. In 2009, we reported that the percentage of plan sponsors adopting autoenrollment had grown from about 1 percent in 2004 to more than 16 percent in 2009.[6] As automatic enrollment increases the number of employees participating in a plan, plan sponsors are likely to incur greater costs for matching employer contributions and for fees paid to plan administrators, and for the increased number of disclosures they are required to send to participants.

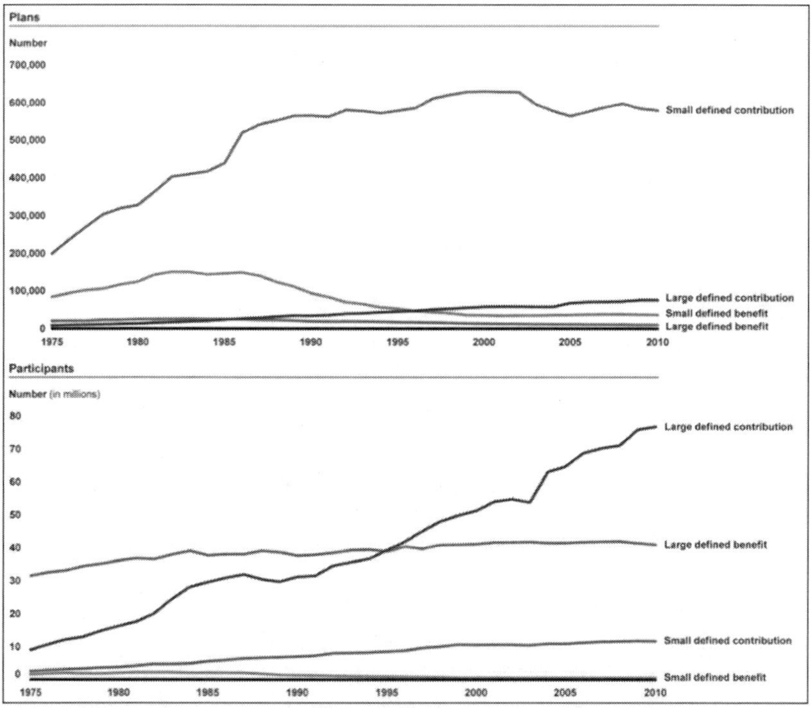

Source: GAO analysis of Form 5500 filings with the U.S. Department of Labor.

Note: Labor's Form 5500 data define small plans as those with 1-99 participants and large plans as those with 100 or more participants. Participants are defined as active employees, retirees, and separated employees with vested benefits.

Figure 1. Number of Pension Plans and Participants, by Plan Size and Type (1975-2010).

Participant Disclosures Required under ERISA

ERISA requires pension plan sponsors[7] to disclose certain material, including reports, statements, notices, and other documents, to participants and other specified individuals. How often plan sponsors must send these disclosures can vary depending on several factors, including whether the disclosure is routine or nonroutine, the type of plan, and the type of information included in the disclosure. Plan sponsors send routine disclosures to participants on a quarterly basis, an annual basis, or over longer periods, depending on the type of plan and filing requirements. A plan sponsor may also be required to send nonroutine disclosures when some type of triggering event occurs to the plan or the participant's circumstances change. Routine and nonroutine disclosures can contain general information about the plan, or personal information, such as a benefit statement or a request for participant action. Table 1 provides examples of some routine and nonroutine disclosures that ERISA requires plan sponsors of DB and DC plans to provide to participants.[8] Some of these disclosures are under Labor's purview, while others are under Treasury's.

Table 1. Examples of Participant Disclosures Required by Law

Disclosure		Information type	Plan types affected
Under Labor's purview			
Routine	Summary plan description 29 U.S.C. § 1021(a)(1).	General	DB[a] and DC[b]
	Summary annual report 29 U.S.C. § 1021(b)(1).	General	DC and someDB
	Annual funding notice 29 U.S.C. § 1021(f)(1).	General	DB
	Participant fee disclosure under ERISA 404(a) 29 CFR 2550. 404a-5.	Personal	DC
	Periodic benefit statement 29 U.S.C. § 1025(a).	Personal	DB and DC
	Notice of qualified default investment alternative 29 U.S.C. §1104(c)(5)(B).	General	Some DC
Nonroutine	Summary of material modifications 29 U.S.C. § 1024(b)(1).	General	DB and DC
	Notice of failure to meet minimum funding standards 29 U.S.C. § 1021(d).	General	DB and someDC
Under Treasury's purview			
Routine	Notice of intent to use safe-harbor formula 26 U.S.C. § 401(k)(12)(D).	General	Some DC
	Notice of qualified automatic contribution arrangement 26 U.S.C. § 401(k)(13)(E)(i).	General	Some DC

Table 1. (Continued)

Disclosure		Information type	Plan types affected
Nonroutine	Notice of significant reduction in future benefit accruals 26 U.S.C. § 4980F(e).	General	DB and someDC
	Suspension of benefits notice 26 U.S.C. § 418E(e)(1).	Personal	Some DB
	Explanation of rollover and certain tax options 26 U.S.C. § 402(f).	Personal	DB and DC

Source: GAO analysis of pension disclosure requirements.

Note: Required disclosures can vary significantly in length; for example, they can range from one page to several hundred pages.

[a] DB = defined benefit plan.

[b] DC = defined contribution plan.

Computer Usage and Internet Access

Employers' use of electronic means to deliver information to employees has grown as the prevalence of computers and Internet access has grown. According to the U.S. Census Current Population Survey, the proportion of households that connect to the Internet at home among heads of household in all age groups and levels of educational attainment has grown over the last decade, including those age 65 or older or with less than a high school education (see fig. 2). Nevertheless, significant proportions of the workforce and the population continue not to have access or participate in mass digital technology. Disparities in household access persist based on age and education level, with older and less educated heads of household less likely to have Internet access in the home, compared with younger and more educated heads of household.

In 2010, only about half of the U.S. population had Internet access at home and about a quarter had Internet access at work, according to data from the most recent panel of the U.S. Census Survey of Income and Program Participation.[9] These data show significant disparities persist among individuals based on a variety of characteristics, including income level, education level, race and ethnicity. For example, about 58 percent of those in the highest income quintile had access to the Internet at work, compared with only about 7 percent of those in the lowest quintile.

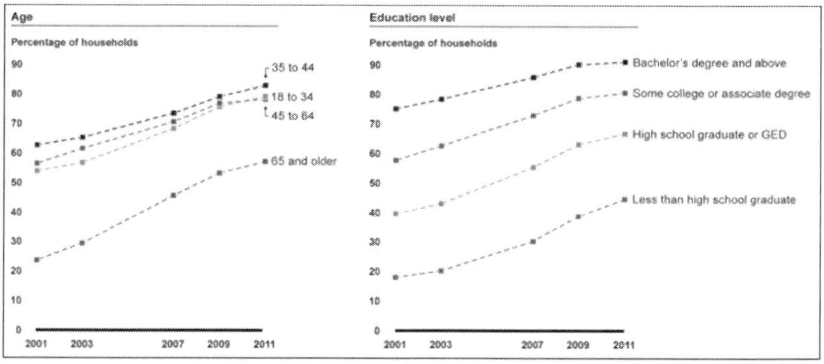

Source: GAO analysis of U.S. Census data.
Note: 2005 data on Internet connectivity were unavailable.

Figure 2. Rising Percentage of Households That Connect to the Internet at Home, by Age and Educational Attainment of Head of Household, 2001-2011.

About 74 percent of individuals with a college degree or higher had Internet access at home compared to 33 percent of individuals with less than a high-school degree. Similarly, the proportion of non-Hispanic individuals with Internet access in the home was more than one-and-one-half the access of Hispanic individuals.

A proliferation of electronic devices, including smart phones, tablets, and laptop computers all capable of accessing digital networks, websites, and information from nearly any location, has made electronic communication commonplace in much of the United States. According to recent surveys on Internet usage, 56 percent of U.S. adults have a smart phone and 34 percent have a tablet computer.[10] This growth in the use of electronic devices and connectivity, however, has not been uniform across all segments of the population. A 2010 industry survey also found that approximately 20 percent of U.S. adults do not use the Internet at all and nearly half of them did not go online because they did not believe the Internet was relevant to them. Most of these non-users also reported that they had never used the Internet before, and did not have anyone in their households who did have access. In addition, 61 percent of these nonusers reported that they would need someone to help them access the Internet.

However, the population of adults who do not use the Internet will likely continue to decline. Census data show that more than 60 percent of 15- to-44-year-olds had Internet access in their homes in 2010. A 2013 study found that many of the disparities in Internet usage found in the adult population (whose reported use of the Internet ranged from 56 to 98 percent), no longer persisted among teens, with about 90 percent of teens in all demographic groups reporting that they use the Internet. [11] (For more detailed data on the characteristics of individuals with and without Internet access, see app. I.)

ELECTRONIC DELIVERY ALLOWED FOR ALL PLAN DISCLOSURES UNDER CERTAIN CIRCUMSTANCES

Federal law and regulations allow sponsors of private pension plans to furnish all pension disclosures to participants electronically under certain circumstances. In some cases, plan sponsors may use electronic delivery as their default delivery method as long as the participants receiving the disclosures meet specific requirements for accessing information electronically. In other cases, plan sponsors must obtain affirmative consent from participants before sending disclosures electronically. Plan sponsors may also furnish certain disclosures on a plan's secure continuous access website. When the criteria for either default delivery or obtaining affirmative consent cannot be met, plan sponsors must mail paper disclosures to participants. In addition, federal regulations require that participants be allowed to request paper disclosures at any time.

Certain Conditions Must Be Met to Implement Electronic Delivery

The Electronic Signatures in Global and National Commerce Act (E-SIGN)[12] provides for the use of electronic disclosure of any information that is required to be in writing, as long as certain conditions concerning consent are met. Certain provisions under ERISA also explicitly specify that sponsors of private pension plans may furnish participant disclosures in written, electronic, or other form as long as they are reasonably accessible.[13] Consistent with these federal laws, regulations pertaining to electronic delivery of plan information to participants were issued by Labor in 2002[14] and by Treasury in 2006.[15] These regulations expanded the scope of electronic delivery to apply to all related ERISA pension plan disclosures under the respective purview of each agency and established standards and procedures to guide the use of electronic delivery. However, the procedures for identifying those participants who qualify for default electronic delivery[16] and those who must provide affirmative consent for electronic delivery can vary depending on which agency has purview over the disclosure, the capacity of the plan sponsor's electronic information system, and the participant's work environment (see fig. 3).

Electronic Signatures in Global and National Commerce Act (E-SIGN)

Enacted on June 30, 2000, E-SIGN facilitates the use of electronic records and signatures in interstate and foreign commerce by generally ensuring the validity and legal effect of transactions entered into electronically. To protect consumers, however, the act provides that if a consumer disclosure is required to be made in writing, the use of an electronic media to deliver it will be valid only if detailed conditions are in place to obtain the consumer's informed consent and ensure that the consumer knows how to also receive the information on paper. For example, consumers must be provided with clear information about how to withdraw their consent as well as the hardware and software necessary to access and retain the information provided electronically. The law also allows federal agencies to make exemptions to these conditions if it is necessary to eliminate a substantial burden on electronic commerce and does not increase the material risk of harm to consumers.

Source: GAO analysis of the E-SIGN statute.

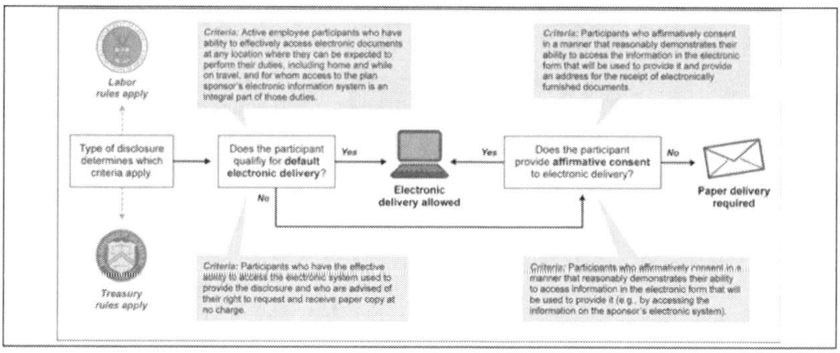

Source: GAO analysis of Labor and Treasury regulations.

Figure 3. Procedures for Identifying Participants Who Qualify for Electronic Delivery.

Electronic Delivery As the Default Delivery Method

Labor and Treasury have structured their regulations quite differently regarding their requirements for sending disclosures to certain participants electronically without consent. Both agencies require, among other things,[17] that in order for plan sponsors to use electronic delivery as the default delivery method, they must identify participants who can effectively access the plan sponsor's electronic information system, but the agencies' criteria for determining effective access vary. Table 2 provides examples of how plan sponsors can meet Labor's and Treasury's different regulatory criteria for default electronic delivery for the disclosures under each agency's purview.

Table 2. Criteria for Allowing Default Electronic Delivery of Disclosures, by Agency

	Labor	*Treasury*
Criteria for default electronic delivery	A plan sponsor can choose to provide required disclosures electronically to any participant who meets the following criteria: Participant has ability to effectively access electronic documents at any location where he or she can be expected to perform his or her duties, including at home and while on travel. AND Participant's access to the employer's or plan sponsor's electronic information system is an integral part of his or her duties. 29 C.F.R. § 2520.104b-1(c)(2)(i) .	A plan sponsor can choose to provide required disclosures electronically to any participant who meets the following criteria: Participant has effective ability to access the electronic system used to provide the disclosure. AND Participant is advised of his or her right to request and receive a paper copy at no charge. 26 C.F.R. § 1.401(a)-21(c).
Descriptive examples	An employee works at a job that requires regular use of a computer to access the employer's e-mail and other electronic systems of the employer to perform his or her duties. The employer e-mail system contains a bounce back feature. If a document bounces back, the plan sponsor follows up to ascertain the problem and if necessary provides the document in paper. The plan sponsor CAN use the employee's work e-mail	An employee works at a job that involves use of a computer. The employer who sponsors a plan CAN use the employee's work e-mail to send disclosures electronically, as long as the employee has the effective ability to access the notice, as determined based, for example, on the employee's receipt of the electronic disclosure. An employee separating from employment provides apersonal e-

	Labor	*Treasury*
	to send ERISA Title I disclosures electronically. An employee separating from employment provides a personal e-mail to the employer as part of the employee's forwarding contact information. The employer who sponsors a plan CANNOT use this personal e-mail to send notices electronically as the default delivery method. An employee provides a personal e-mail to the employer as part of the employee's emergency contact information. The employer who sponsors a plan CANNOT use this personal e-mail to send notices electronically as the default delivery method.	mail to the employer as part of the employee's forwarding contact information. The employer who sponsors a plan CAN use this personal e-mail to send notices electronically, as longas the employee has the ability to effectively access the notice, as determined based, for example, on the employee having provided the e-mail address and/or receipt of the electronic notice. An employee provides a personal e-mail to the employer as part of the employee's emergency contact information. The employer who sponsors a plan CAN use this personal e-mail to send notices electronically, as long as the employee has the ability to effectively access the notice, as determined based on the employee having provided the e-mail address and/or receipt of the electronic notice.

Source: GAO analysis of Labor and Treasury regulations.

Labor's notice of final rulemaking indicated that the agency's regulations were designed to be consistent with the goals of E-SIGN and to facilitate the voluntary use of electronic records while ensuring continued accuracy, integrity, and accessibility of employee benefit plan information and records required to be kept by law.[18] Labor's electronic disclosure regulations require pension plan sponsors to take appropriate and necessary measures reasonably calculated to ensure that the system for furnishing documents results in actual receipt of transmitted information and protects personal account and benefit information.[19] If the system for furnishing documents does not include appropriate and necessary measures that are reasonably calculated to ensure actual receipt of electronically furnished documents, the plan sponsor must furnish the disclosure through a nonelectronic medium, such as paper. These regulations establish a safe harbor for plan sponsors to use electronic delivery as the default delivery method as long as the employee uses the electronic information system as an integral part of their work duties. According to Labor, this safe harbor applies to furnishing electronic disclosures to actively employed participants, including those who work at home or who may be on travel as long as they have "ready access" there to the employer's electronic information system.[20] In addition, by definition, this safe harbor limits use of electronic delivery as the default delivery method to actively employed participants only; former employees, retirees, and beneficiaries are effectively excluded, and must either provide their consent to electronic delivery or receive paper disclosures.

Treasury's regulations are also designed to comply with the requirements of E-SIGN, [21] but Treasury's regulations establish somewhat different criteria than Labor for allowing pension plan sponsors to use electronic delivery as the default delivery method for participant disclosures under Treasury's purview. Under E-SIGN federal agencies may create exemptions to these conditions if it is necessary to eliminate a substantial burden on electronic commerce and does not increase the material risk of harm to consumers.[22] In general, a plan sponsor may use default electronic delivery to participants who demonstrate an ability to use the hardware or software used to provide the disclosure. For example, if a participant requested a distribution on a plan's website after entering protected identifying information and an e-mail address to which a disclosure was to be sent, a plan sponsor who sent a disclosure via email, and requested and received automatic notification that the participant opened the e-mail, would meet the disclosure requirements. However, if a plan sponsor sent an e-mail and did not receive a return receipt, the plan sponsor could not ensure the disclosure requirements are being met.[23] In addition, as is the case under Labor's regulations, participants who are defaulted to electronic delivery under Treasury's regulations may request paper copies of any notice sent electronically, but they must submit their requests for paper on a document-by-document basis.[24]

Obtaining Participant Consent for Electronic Delivery

Labor and Treasury regulations also allow pension plan sponsors to send electronic disclosures to other participants who do not qualify for default electronic delivery but provide their affirmative consent. Each agency established separate criteria for plan sponsors to use to obtain participant consent (see table 3).

Table 3. Criteria for Obtaining Affirmative Consent for Electronic Delivery of Disclosures, by Agency

	Labor	*Treasury*
Criteria for obtaining affirmative consent	A plan sponsor must seek affirmative consent from participants before sending any notices electronically. A plan sponsor delivers to participants an initial notice about the documents to which consent would apply, their right to withdraw consent at any time and receive paper copies, and the procedures for updating their contact information. Participant provides affirmative consent to receiving documents electronically in a manner reasonably demonstrating ability to access information in electronic form and provides an e-mail address. Plan sponsors are only required to reaffirm participant consent if they change the information system's hardware or software requirements. 29 C.F.R. § 2520.104b-1(c)(2)(ii).	A plan sponsor must seek affirmative consent from participants before sending any notices electronically. A plan sponsor delivers to participants an initial notice about the documents to which consent would apply, theirright to withdraw consent at any time and receive paper copies, and the procedures for updating their contact information. Participant provides affirmative consent to receiving documents electronically in a manner reasonably demonstrating the ability to access the electronic system used to deliver the notice. For example, once a participant accesses the system, the plan sponsor may send disclosures electronically. Plan sponsors are only required to reaffirm participant consent if they change the information system's hardware or software requirements. 26 C.F.R. § 1.401(a)-21(b)(2)(i).
Descriptive examples	After delivering to a participant the initial notice, a plan sponsor mails or e-mails a notice with instructions on how to consent to electronic delivery of plan information. By following these instructions, the participant affirmatively consents to electronic delivery.	A plan sponsor e-mails a notice containing an attached file (e.g., an application, spreadsheet, or web link) that will be used to deliver plan information. If a participant opens the attachment, selects the consent button, and returns the attachment, this constitutes affirmative consent to electronic delivery through that electronic medium. A plan sponsor can also mail a paper notice with instructions on how to access the electronic medium. If aparticipant successfully accesses the information systemand indicates

Table 3. (Continued)

	Labor	*Treasury*
		consent, this constitutes affirmative consent to electronic delivery through that electronic medium.

Source: GAO analysis of Labor and Treasury regulations.

Both Labor's and Treasury's regulations require plans seeking to obtain affirmative consent to provide participants with an initial notice explaining certain rights. Among other things, this notice must identify the scope of the consent (e.g., whether it applies to one notice or all subsequent notices), a participant's right to withdraw consent at any time, and procedures for withdrawing consent and for updating information needed to contact the participant electronically. While Labor's regulations require participants who choose to consent to electronic delivery to provide an email address,[25] Treasury regulations do not. Specifically, Treasury's regulations allow plan sponsors to rely on whatever e-mail they may have for a participant. If a participant accesses a notice sent to him or her, selects a consent button on the notice, and then returns the notice through the sponsor's electronic information system used to deliver this notice—that is sufficient to constitute affirmative consent. Under both regulations, plan sponsors must develop a process for requesting and recording whether consent was obtained from each participant.

Posting to a Secure Website

In 2006, Labor issued general guidance [26] that addressed the requirement for pension plan sponsors to furnish periodic pension benefit statements to participants. The Labor guidance included provisions stating that plan sponsors wishing to furnish pension benefit statements to participants electronically could (1) determine participant eligibility for electronic delivery following either the Treasury or Labor rules or (2) make the statements available on a secure continuous access website,[27] as long as the plan sponsor provided certain information to the participant (either electronically or by paper) prior to posting the statement online. The guidance also stated that a plan sponsor must, in any case, notify participants that the statement is available, provide instructions on how to access the statement online, and apprise participants of their right to request and obtain a paper version of the current statement free of charge. To furnish the statements this way, a plan sponsor would need to notify participants—either electronically or on paper—

that the statement is available. Participants would either follow a web link provided in the notice or manually access the plan's website. The participant would be prompted to enter a username and password in order to access the statements. Participants not wanting to access their statements electronically would have to follow instructions on the notice to request a paper copy of the current statement, such as by contacting a call center after the receipt of a notice.

Paper Delivery Required for Some Participants

When neither the default electronic delivery nor the affirmative consent criteria can be met, pension plan sponsors must mail paper disclosures to participants. Federal regulations and guidance governing electronic delivery underscore the importance of protecting a participant's right to request and receive paper disclosures from their pension plans. When promulgating its electronic delivery regulations in 2002, Labor acknowledged that electronic disclosures may not accommodate the needs of every participant on every occasion for a variety of reasons, such as malfunctioning hardware or software, and readability and portability. Therefore, preserving participants' ability to receive paper versions of electronically furnished documents is important to ensuring adequate disclosure to participants.[28] Labor's and Treasury's regulations both require that all participants receiving notices electronically be notified of their right to request documents in paper at any time, and without exception, plan sponsors are required to provide participants with paper disclosures upon request.

VARIOUS ADVANTAGES AND DISADVANTAGES REPORTED CONCERNING THE USE OF ELECTRONIC DELIVERY

Industry representatives and participant advocates we spoke with agreed that the popularity of electronic delivery was growing due to various efficiencies—such as reduced costs and better tracking of disclosures— that can be advantageous for some pension plan sponsors and participants.[29] However, both groups also raised various concerns with the requirements associated with electronic delivery, citing issues with their lack of consistency and clarity as well as concerns that they may not adequately protect participant choice for those who need or prefer to receive paper.

Reported Advantages of Electronic Delivery

Reduced Costs

A major impetus for expanding electronic disclosure is its ability to reduce plan sponsors' costs. Industry representatives and participant advocates we spoke with agreed that electronic delivery could reduce plan costs by decreasing the amount of paper needed for disclosures, and by rolling back the level of printing and mailing required of paper delivery. In its 2002 regulations, Labor estimated that use of electronic delivery would reduce plan sponsors' printing, materials, and mailing costs associated with relevant ERISA disclosures by approximately 14 percent in the first year of implementation and result in tens of millions of dollars in annual savings in subsequent years.[30] One industry representative estimated that mailing a one-page document—including the paper, postage, and envelope—costs, on average, about 53 cents. In contrast, the average estimated cost to send the same document electronically, including the posting of the file and issuing an e-mail notifying the individual of the document's availability, was less than 1 cent. One service provider that administered accounts for approximately 9 million participants told us that it could cost up to $15 to print and deliver a 500-page paper summary plan description to each participant. In contrast, sending this disclosure electronically to all participants could result in millions of dollars in savings in the form of significant reductions in administrative costs for the plan.[31] Industry representatives and participant advocates also acknowledged that, in addition to cost savings for plans, electronic delivery can result in numerous environmental benefits including reductions in the use of paper, print products, and fuel used to deliver paper disclosures to participants through the U.S. mail.

Built-in Tracking

Another advantage of electronic delivery is that pension plan sponsors' information systems have the built-in capacity to track the delivery of electronic disclosures. According to industry representatives, plan sponsors can track the receipt of electronic notices using the delivery and read receipt functions of their existing e-mail systems.[32] For example, they said that some plan sponsors track and monitor the extent to which they successfully deliver electronic notices to participants and can monitor how many participants access the plan's website after opening and reading an e-mail notification. Tracking the receipt of e-mail notices allows plan sponsors to confirm whether a participant received the e-mail. If an e-mail bounces back as undeliverable, one service provider told us that this activates automatic paper delivery as a safety net and sends a paper notice to the participant's last known address. Plan sponsors can also use existing systems to monitor more participant responses to certain disclosures better than is possible using paper delivery. For example, plan sponsors can track the rate at which participants use web links embedded in their electronic disclosures to access their online pension accounts or available online retirement management tools. Although such tracking capability exists, plan sponsors are not required to use this capability to ensure that participants open disclosures sent electronically.[33] Industry representatives said that such a requirement would require plan sponsors using electronic delivery to incur the costs of taking the additional steps of tracking and documenting receipt for electronic delivery—steps that are not required for plan sponsors using paper delivery. Moreover, they noted that tracking the receipt of notices sent electronically cannot ensure that a participant actually reads the notice. Participant advocates suggested that the costs incurred by plan sponsors would be minimal and a requirement that plan sponsors use existing technology and e-mail systems to track which documents were opened would provide some assurance of actual receipt.

Improved Access and Archiving

One further advantage of electronic delivery is that it offers participants who receive electronic disclosures improved access to their most current retirement information and better archiving capability, according to both industry representatives and participant advocates. For example, electronic delivery can provide participants with greater access to their retirement information since it is always available on the plan sponsor's website or electronic archive. Participants can also access the information from any location with a working Internet connection and archive disclosures more efficiently.

For example, participants can download disclosures to their electronic devices in Portable Document Format (PDF) for electronic filing at any time and from any location. Industry representatives reported that some plan sponsors provide participants with secure online storage accounts where they can archive disclosures.

Industry representatives also reported that electronic delivery offers other efficiencies related to access, such as improved delivery times for disclosures and greater accuracy and timeliness of retirement information provided on account statements and plan documents. For example, plan sponsors who use electronic delivery can provide nearly real-time retirement information and account balances on a participant's statement, and can include the most up-to-date provisions in the summary plan description posted to the plan's website or as a PDF file attached to an email.

Participant advocates supported the concept of an online electronic archive that contained all plan notices so that participants could easily locate the information they needed when they needed it.

Increased Participant Choice of Electronic Communication

Electronic delivery offers participants a choice of delivery methods and aligns with the needs of a growing sector of the population, according to both industry representatives and participant advocates we interviewed. Participant advocates acknowledged that there are situations, such as in industries that employ a young professional workforce, in which electronic delivery is preferable to plans and participants, especially when a participant has elected to receive information electronically.

One large service provider who monitors participant delivery preferences told us that the proportion of participants communicating electronically with the firm had grown in the past several years from about 40 percent to about 60 percent, and that 91 percent of its DC plan participants conducted transactions using the Internet compared to 9 percent who conducted transactions over the telephone.

In 2012, another large service provider who administered accounts for approximately 20 million participants reported that 60 percent of participants in plans with paper as the default delivery method opted to receive their statements electronically. Another service provider reported that, among participants in smaller plans, the number of participants opting into electronic delivery had increased significantly in the last 3 years, from just under 22,500 participants in 2010 to nearly 140,000 participants in 2012, with 46 percent of its total participants opting to receive statements electronically.[34]

REPORTED DISADVANTAGES OF ELECTRONIC DELIVERY REQUIREMENTS

Default Criteria Too Complex

According to some industry representatives, more plan sponsors—both large and small—would like to take advantage of efficiencies associated with electronic disclosure, but given the complexity of the requirements for default electronic disclosure, they are fearful of misinterpreting some aspect of these criteria or being found in noncompliance. In particular, they told us that they find the criteria for meeting Labor's "integral part of duties" safe harbor threshold especially challenging, especially with respect to how these criteria apply to employees who perform their duties at a field location. They noted that while these employees may have ready access to the plan sponsor's information system, the extent to which an employee must regularly access the employer's electronic information system to qualify for the safe harbor is unclear. Without specific standards that clearly describe the requirements for these kinds of scenarios, industry representatives told us that some plan sponsors were reluctant to use electronic delivery as the default delivery method, opting instead to reduce their risk of noncompliance either by seeking affirmative consent from their employees for electronic disclosure or by providing only paper disclosures. In contrast, participant advocates did not agree with the industry representatives' point of view. They told us that when compared to Treasury's criteria for default delivery, in their view, Labor's integral part of duties safe harbor requirements struck a good balance between protecting a participant's rights to paper disclosures and permitting plan sponsors to use electronic delivery.

Further, industry representatives told us that in general the criteria can be cumbersome to apply. For example, one plan sponsor told us that although the company's workforce was highly technical and therefore more likely than not to use the plan sponsor's information system to conduct an integral part of their duties, there were exceptions. As a result, the plan sponsor had to conduct a thorough review of all business operations and employee classifications, and monitor its workforce's access to computers on an ongoing basis as businesses opened or closed. If there were any doubt as to an employee's qualifications for default electronic delivery, the plan sponsor would exclude that employee from automatic e-disclosure and default to paper delivery.[35] Industry representatives also told us that plan sponsors were hesitant to attempt default electronic delivery for disclosures under Labor's purview because the requirements lack clarity as to how the "integral part of duties" safe harbor applies to nonstandard work situations. For example, as noted earlier, some plan sponsors may have many employees who work outside the office and use their personal computer once a day to access the plan sponsor's electronic information system to check their schedule, input orders, and review e-mail. Industry representatives told us that they thought this level of computer use is integral for these employees to successfully carry out their duties and it likely met the safe harbor threshold, but a number of plan sponsors were reportedly reluctant to use default delivery in such cases because it was unclear whether this met Labor's threshold. To realize the efficiencies of electronic delivery as use of electronic communication grows, industry representatives told us that many plan sponsors would like to use electronic delivery as their default delivery method for all disclosures for any participants whose working e-mail address was on file, with an opt-out provision for those that prefer paper. Labor officials, however, questioned whether the pension marketplace should be setting the precedent in moving to electronic default notification systems. They noted that banks, insurance companies, and mutual fund companies are not establishing electronic default notification systems for their customers, but instead are allowing customers to opt into electronic delivery if they choose. Participant advocates we spoke with did not support efforts to make electronic delivery the default method for all disclosures sent to all participants, saying that such a move would likely deny access to plan information for significant numbers of participants who did not have Internet access.

Inadequate Participant Protections

According to industry representatives, the regulatory requirements for furnishing disclosures on a plan's secure continuous access website are too restrictive in that only two disclosures qualify. Plan sponsors told us that they would like to use this medium to furnish other required disclosures and plan information. [36] Specifically, they noted that allowing plan sponsors to expand the use of their websites to furnish disclosures that contain general plan information, such as a summary annual report, would significantly reduce plan administrative costs. In contrast, the participant advocates we spoke with had mixed views on this idea. Some agreed with the industry representatives, noting that it made sense to allow plan sponsors to furnish certain general information disclosures on a plan sponsor's website. However, others disagreed, saying that a secure website, unlike paper, could not ensure that all participants could access plan information. Several participant advocates expressed concerns that the Treasury's rules for default electronic delivery do not adequately safeguard a participant's ability to choose to receive paper disclosures. Specifically, they were concerned that these requirements give pension plan sponsors too much discretion to determine whether participants have the effective ability to access the plan sponsor's electronic system and receive disclosures electronically. According to participant advocates, the lack of an affirmative consent requirement for these disclosures could prove problematic for participants who may inadvertently have demonstrated their effective ability to access electronic communication at some point in the past and may be unaware that plan sponsors are sending electronic notices to an old or unused e-mail address. In these situations, plan sponsors would only know that the disclosure was not reaching the participant if the e-mail bounced back as undeliverable. Several participant advocates also expressed concern that over the course of a career some participants who affirmatively consented to electronic delivery may forget the choice they made, resulting in failure to receive key retirement disclosures.[37] This can be especially problematic for spouses and beneficiaries after a participant's death. According to participant advocates, spouses and beneficiaries may not even know that a deceased participant earned a benefit or provided affirmative consent to receive disclosures electronically. For example, officials at one service provider told us that they would continue to send disclosures electronically to an e-mail address after the participant has separated from employment or retired, if they had a working e-mail address on file.[38] In such a situation, spouses and beneficiaries could potentially lose connection to their benefit after the participant's death unless they were aware of the participant's personal e-mail account and knew how to access it. Industry representatives and participant advocates alike stressed the importance of safeguarding participant choice of delivery method to ensure that all participants with a retirement account can access plan information. To accomplish this, they noted that paper delivery would remain necessary for some time. While national data on participant preferences for how plans communicate plan information are limited, a 2012 survey of a national sample of participants found that a majority of participants at all ages preferred to receive plan information on paper. [39] At the same time, both industry representatives and participant advocates acknowledged that choice applies to both paper and electronic delivery methods and that each delivery method has a range of pros and cons that may be weighed differently by different participants (see fig. 4).

	Paper delivery		Electronic delivery	
	Pros	Cons	Pros	Cons
Default delivery	If prefer paper, no extra effort required to obtain disclosure	If prefer electronic, extra steps may be required to obtain electronically (if available)	If prefer electronic, no extra steps required	If prefer paper, extra steps required to obtain paper
Access and archiving	Paper notices, once received, are available any time Easier for spouses and beneficiaries to maintain access	Requires extra steps and physical space to store Notices can be misplaced	Electronic notices, once received, are available any time No extra steps or physical space required to store in an organized manner	May lose access to notices if computer malfunctions or Internet connection is lost Harder for spouses and beneficiaries to maintain access
Receipt	Low risk of post office failing to deliver notice or delivering to unoccupied home	Delivery (and return if undeliverable) could take days or weeks Could get lost among participant's other mail No guarantee that received paper notice will be read	Delivery and return (bounce-back) of undeliverable notices is immediate	If bounces back, notice has to be re-sent by mail If delivered to unused account or blocked by spam filter, would not be identified as undeliverable Could get lost among participant's other email No guarantee that received electronic notice will be read
Cost	No direct costs to participants	Costs of printing and mailing for sponsors could add to indirect costs that are passed on to participants	No costs of printing and mailing that could add to indirect costs passed on to participants Less paper consumed/better for environment	Costs of printing electronic notices incurred by participants Participant incurs costs of maintaining computer, software, and Internet connection
Security	No extra steps required to ensure security	Vulnerable to security breach if mail is lost or stolen	Passwords can help protect personal information[a]	Vulnerable to security breach from hacking[b] or phishing[c]
Personalization	N/A	Cannot adjust font size to improve readability or use links to access other related documents or tools (including translation tools for non-English speakers and narration tools for the blind)	Can adjust font size to improve readability or use links to access other related documents or tools (including translation tools for non-English speakers and narration tools for the blind)	N/A

Source: GAO analysis of Labor data and interviews with agency officials, industry representatives and participant advocacy groups.

[a] Pension plan sponsors also employ additional countermeasures to protect participant information online by using encryption software and firewalls to increase the security of plan websites, and in some cases, by requiring participants to answer security questions or to validate their computer's Internet protocol address before allowing access to online retirement accounts.

[b] We recently reported that federal agencies have seen increasing numbers of cybersecurity incidents that have placed sensitive information at risk, with potentially serious impacts on federal and military operations; critical infrastructure; and the confidentiality, integrity, and availability of sensitive government, private sector, and personal information. The increasing risks are demonstrated by the dramatic increase in reports of security incidents, the ease of obtaining and using hacking tools, and steady advances in the sophistication and effectiveness of attack technology. See GAO, Cybersecurity: National Strategy, Roles, and Responsibilities Need to Be Better Defined and More Effectively Implemented, GAO-13-187 (Washington, D.C.: Feb. 14, 2013). In addition, the Federal Trade Commission has reported that consumer complaints about identify theft were the most frequent form of complaint filed in 2012, accounting for 18 percent of all consumer complaints filed that year. Individuals age 50 or older filed just over a third of these complaints (98,100). Consumers also reported that e-mail was the most common method of contact used to initiate fraud.

[c] The Department of Justice has described phishing as luring techniques that identity thieves use to fish for personal information of unsuspecting Internet users to perpetrate fraud. Phishing often involves the use of deceptive websites or e-mail to trick Internet users into disclosing their bank and financial information or other personal data such as usernames and passwords. It is estimated phishing attacks have resulted in global losses of billions of dollars.

Figure 4. Pros and Cons That May Affect a Participant's Choice of Delivery Method for Pension Disclosures.

As the popularity of electronic communication grows, the demand for electronic disclosures will also grow. Facilitating electronic delivery to meet future growing demand also serves to safeguard participant choice for those participants who prefer electronic communication but currently cannot exercise this preference.[40]

Certain Electronic Disclosure Requirements Are Somewhat Inconsistent and Unclear, and May Not Fully Protect Participant Choice

Our examination of the regulations and guidance related to the concerns raised by industry representatives and participant groups identified several weaknesses in the agencies' requirements related to electronic disclosure. For example, we found the requirements describing which participants qualify for electronic delivery to be somewhat inconsistent and unclear, especially with respect to requirements for default electronic delivery and obtaining affirmative consent. In addition, we found that the requirements permitting default electronic delivery to furnish disclosures may not fully protect participants' ability to choose a preferred delivery method or revisit this choice when their circumstances change.

Requirements for Default Electronic Delivery Are Somewhat Inconsistent and Unclear

Federal agencies are to draft regulations that are easy to understand with the goal of minimizing the potential for uncertainty and avoid regulations that are inconsistent or incompatible with regulations of other agencies.[41] Our analysis of the regulations governing the use of electronic disclosure found, as was indicated in our interviews with industry representatives, that the regulatory requirements for determining which participants qualify for default electronic delivery are somewhat lacking in consistency and clarity.

Labor's and Treasury's regulations governing electronic disclosure set different standards for plan sponsors to follow for using default electronic delivery. Specifically, to ensure compliance with Treasury's requirements for default electronic delivery, plan sponsors need to monitor participants' ability to access the electronic information system. On the other hand, to ensure compliance with Labor's default disclosure requirements, plan sponsors need to monitor changes in the work status and computer access of their active employees to ensure that employees continue to meet these regulatory criteria of (1) having the effective ability to access their employer's information system; (2) using this system as an integral part of their duties; and (3) conducting their work from a worksite with ready access to the system. If an employee's work status changed and no longer met the Labor threshold, the plan sponsor would need to discontinue default electronic delivery to this participant. These regulatory schemes are not necessarily incompatible; plan sponsors could simultaneously comply with both. The fact that the requirements are different could mean that some sponsors would need to develop different compliance strategies for each.

This issue becomes of particular concern in nonstandard work situations where employees may not have ready access to their computers. Our analysis of the Labor requirements found that while they do offer some flexibility with regard to alternative worksites, they could be clearer about the thresholds qualifying employees must meet. Specifically, Labor's regulations describe an employee's worksite as "any location where a participant is reasonably expected to perform his or her duties as an employee,"[42] and this description includes "employees who work at home or who may be on travel, provided they have ready access to the employer's information system."[43] Labor officials told us that employees who worked in the field (such as salespeople, delivery workers, or telecommuters) would likely meet the safe harbor criteria because the actual location of an employee's work was less important than the expectation that an employee would have ready access to the employer's electronic information system and would likely receive timely notice of any disclosures. However, we found that the regulations do not contain this level of specification or provide clear examples of how plan sponsors can determine whether an employee meets the "integral part of duties" threshold of having ready access to the employer's electronic information system.

Certain Requirements May Not Fully Protect Participant Choice

ERISA's overall reporting and disclosure framework is intended to assure, among other things, that participants in private pension plans are provided or have access to sufficient information to protect their rights and benefits under the plans. To help assure sufficient access, both Labor's and Treasury's regulations safeguard participant choice in how disclosures are delivered by requiring plan sponsors to send paper documents to participants upon request. However, in light of participant concerns in this area, we examined the regulations related to participant choice and identified certain weaknesses in the current regulatory structure. Specifically, we found that participants are not allowed to easily opt out of all default electronic delivery entirely, but must request paper on a document-by-document basis. We also found that participants are afforded limited opportunities to revisit participant consent. While neither of these weaknesses represents a failure to protect participant choice, as participants have the right to request paper copies of disclosures at any time, strengthening the regulatory structure in these areas could better ensure that participants receive information in a timely way by their preferred delivery method.

No Opportunity to Opt out of Default Electronic Delivery

Neither Labor's nor Treasury's requirements for permitting default electronic delivery include provisions that give participants the choice of opting out of all electronic disclosures entirely. Although some plan sponsors may make such an option available, they are not required to do so. As mentioned earlier in this report, both Labor's and Treasury's regulations[44] require plan sponsors to make paper versions of electronically furnished documents available to participants and beneficiaries upon request. However, Labor and Treasury officials confirmed that under these provisions, in situations where plan sponsors do not allow participants to opt out of electronic delivery entirely, participants wanting paper documents can only request a paper copy of a disclosure on a document-by-document basis, which is more tedious and time-consuming for both participants and plans sponsors than an arrangement that would permit participants to exercise the choice to opt out of electronic disclosures entirely.[45] We also found that Labor's 2006 general guidance requires plan sponsors to apprise participants of their right to request and obtain a paper version of their current benefit statement free of charge, but does not require them to allow participants to opt out entirely of receiving their statements electronically in this manner.[46] Therefore, participants wanting paper copies of their quarterly benefit statement or quarterly fee information would need to request a paper copy from the plan each time a new statement became available on the plan's website. In these situations, participants would have no ability to change their preferred delivery method for how they wished to receive information about their retirement accounts on an ongoing basis.

Few Opportunities to Revisit Consent

Our analysis also found that under the current requirements for electronic disclosure, plan sponsors are required to notify participants of their rights to withdraw consent for electronic delivery, but they are not required to revisit participant consent for electronic delivery except under limited circumstances. Specifically, both Labor's and Treasury's regulations require plan sponsors, prior to obtaining participant consent, to notify participants of their right to withdraw their consent for electronic delivery at any time. However, the regulations do not require plan sponsors to remind participants of this right, or to reconfirm participants' preferences, except under certain, limited circumstances, such as when plan sponsors make a change to their hardware or software that could affect participants' access.[47] Having requirements that sponsors provide such reminders would help ensure that participants, who may prefer paper disclosures or who do not have the proper hardware or software to receive electronic disclosures, have the opportunity to register a preference in how they wish to receive plan information.

CONCLUSION

The ultimate purpose of the ERISA disclosure requirements is to ensure that participants can access information about their pension plans when they need it in order to help them make informed decisions about their retirement. To this end, efforts to facilitate the broader use of electronic delivery must be accompanied by efforts to safeguard participants' right to receive paper disclosures, if they so choose. Much has changed in the workplace since Labor and Treasury issued their respective final electronic disclosure regulations. Advances in technology in the areas of digital communication, and widespread use of the Internet at work and at home have redefined the workplace. In addition, the broad adoption of new technologies, such as remote access and secure continuous access websites, has made it possible for employees to conduct their work and access information any time from any location with Internet access. Yet the regulatory requirements for determining which participants qualify for default electronic delivery are somewhat inconsistent and unclear, leaving some plan sponsors uncertain as to how to apply the requirements to their participants. In addition, participants defaulted into electronic delivery may have few opportunities to express their preferences for how they receive plan information, increasing the risk that they will not get information in a way that best serves their needs. The transition underway towards greater use of electronic disclosure has the potential to achieve benefits for plan sponsors and participants in the form of reduced costs and greater access. At the same time, paper disclosures continue to play an important role in meeting the needs of those not connected to the Internet or who prefer paper, and in helping locate participants when e-mail communications are returned as undeliverable. For these reasons, it is essential that plan sponsors maintain the capacity to provide paper disclosures even if the bulk of their disclosures move to electronic format over time, and that a participant's right to choose to receive paper disclosures is strengthened and protected.

Recommendations for Executive Action

We recommend that the Secretary of Labor and the Secretary of the Treasury take the following three actions:

1) Work together to develop clear and consistent requirements for default electronic delivery of pension-related disclosures.
2) Consider requiring pension plan sponsors to provide participants with an opportunity to opt out of all forms of electronic delivery, including (but not limited to) disclosures sent by default electronic delivery and disclosures posted on a secure continuous access website.
3) Consider requiring pension plan sponsors to send a periodic paper notice to participants reminding them of their right to change their preferred delivery method at any time and the steps they must take to make these changes.

Agency Comments and Our Evaluation

We provided a draft of this report to Labor, Treasury, and the Pension Benefit Guaranty Corporation for review. Only Labor provided formal written comments. Labor generally agreed with our findings and recommendations. In its comments, Labor emphasized its view that employees are in the best position to determine the method of delivery that is most effective in communicating plan information to them. Moreover, Labor said that it would continue to seek to foster delivery systems that both protect a participant's right to get required information while offering plans flexibility to use electronic disclosure to achieve efficiencies. In addition, all three agencies provided technical comments, which we incorporated in the report, as appropriate.

Charles A. Jeszeck, Director
Education, Workforce, and Income Security Issues

APPENDIX I: INTERNET ACCESS FOR INDIVIDUALS AGE 15 AND OLDER, BY SELECTED CHARACTERISTICS (2010)

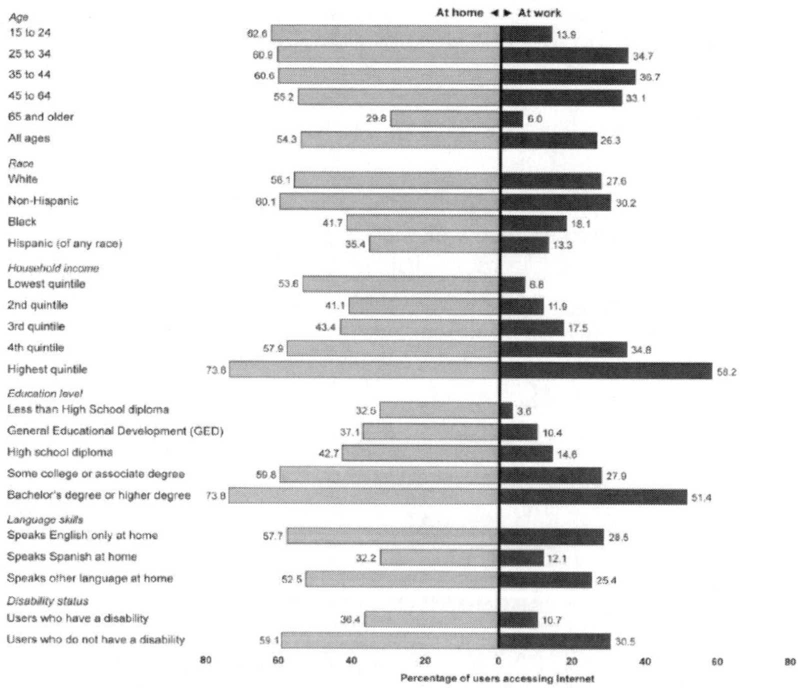

Soure: U.S. Census Bureau, 2008 SIPP Panel.

End Notes

[1] Pub. L. No. 93-406, 88 Stat. 829 (codified in part at 29 U.S.C. §§ 1002 -1461).

[2] Exec. Order No. 13,563, 76 Fed. Reg. 3,821 (Jan. 21, 2011) (calling on federal agencies to retrospectively consider existing policies to seek to achieve regulatory goals using the most innovative and least burdensome tools).

[3] Request for Information Regarding Electronic Disclosure by Employee Benefit Plans, 76 Fed. Reg. 19,285 (Apr. 7, 2011). Labor received 78 responses to its 2011 request for information. Labor officials said that they continue to review these and have made no decision as to whether the department will issue new regulations on electronic disclosure.

[4] Under ERISA, DB and DC plans are referred to as pension plans rather than retirement plans. 29 U.S.C. § 1002(34) and (35).

[5] Pub. L. No. 109-280, § 902, 120 Stat. 780, 1033-39. In addition, PPA extended liability protections to plans when participants provide plans with no direction about the investment of their funds, as may be more apt to happen in cases of autoenrollment. § 624, 120 Stat. 980.

[6] GAO, Retirement Savings: Automatic Enrollment Shows Promise for Some Workers, but Proposals to Broaden Retirement Savings for Other Workers Could Face Challenges, GAO-10-31 (Washington, D.C.: Oct. 23, 2009).

[7] The plan sponsor is ultimately responsible for ensuring that the plan complies with all legal requirements whether it is done directly or through third parties. Therefore, we use the term "plan sponsor" broadly throughout this report to refer to plan administrators, fiduciaries, or other service providers who may provide reports and disclosures on behalf of a plan sponsor.

[8] We are conducting a separate study on the extent of reporting and disclosure requirements for private-sector plans, scheduled to be issued later this year.

[9] U.S. Census Bureau, Survey of Income and Program Participation, 2008 Panel. (Internet release date June 2012) http://www.census.gov/hhes/computer/publications/2010.html.

[10] Pew Research Center Internet & American Life Project, Spring Tracking Survey, April 17-May 19, 2013, accessed on July 2, 2013, http://www.pewinternet.org/StaticPages/Trend-Data-%28Adults%29/Whos-Online.aspx. It is likely that some of the individuals surveyed had multiple devices.

[11] Pew Research Center Internet & American Life Project, Teens and Privacy Management Survey, July 26-Sept. 30, 2012, accessed on July 2, 2013, http://www.pewinternet.org/Static-Pages/Trend-Data-%28Teens%29/Whos-Online.aspx. Some of this access may be at school or other location, and may not signify that these teens have home or continuous access. However, it does indicate a rapid increase in familiarity with electronic communication among this generation.

[12] Pub. L. No. 106-229, 114 Stat 464, codified at 15 U.S.C. §§ 7001-7006.

[13] For example, 29 U.S.C. §§ 1021(f)(4)(C) (annual funding notice) and 1025(a)(2)(A)(4) (periodic benefit statement).

[14] Final Rules Relating to Use of Electronic Communication and Recordkeeping Technologies by Employee Pension and Welfare Benefit Plans, 67 Fed. Reg. 17,264 (Apr. 9, 2002).

[15] Use of Electronic Media for Providing Employee Benefit Notices and Making Employee Benefit Elections and Consents, 71 Fed. Reg. 61,877 (Oct. 20, 2006).

[16] Throughout this report, we use the term "default electronic delivery" to refer to the conditions under which plan sponsor may provide notices to participants electronically without obtaining participant consent.

[17] For example, both agencies require electronic disclosures to include notification of the significance of the information provided and that the recipient has a right to request and receive the material in paper form. 29 C.F.R. § 2520.104b-1(c)(1)(iii) and 26 C.F.R. § 1.401(a)-21(a)(5)(ii)).

[18] 67 Fed. Reg. 17,269.

[19] 29 CFR § 2520.104b–1(c)(1)(i). One method that a plan sponsor could use to ensure actual receipt would be the use of an automatic read receipt feature in the e-mail software. When the recipient opens the e-mail, an automatic notification would be sent to the plan sponsor that the e-mail was received and opened. Another method would be to require all undeliverable e-mail messages be returned, or "bounced back," thereby alerting the plan sponsor that the e-mail address that they have for a participant is no longer valid. Still another method would be for the administrator to use periodic reviews or surveys to confirm that the employer's e-mail system results in actual receipt.

[20] 67 Fed. Reg. 17,265.

[21] 71 Fed. Reg. 61,877.

[22] § 104(b)(1), 114 Stat. 469 (codified at 15 U.S.C. § 7004(b)(1)).

[23] Treasury's regulations do not include a rule under which an e-mail sent to the last known e-mail address would be deemed to have been successfully delivered. 71 Fed. Reg. 61, 881.A disclosure that is "provided" in a manner consistent with Treasury's electronic delivery requirements will meet a requirement that the disclosure be in writing, but merely because it may meet the "in writing" requirement does not mean that the plan sponsor met the requirement to provide the notice to the recipient. Treasury officials noted that this is important because, for example, a plan sponsor that keeps sending notices to a participant's e-mail address after receiving a notification that the messages are undeliverable cannot be said to have met its legal obligation to provide that notice.

[24] 26 C.F.R. § 1.401(a)-21(c)(3).

[25] 29 C.F.R. § 2520.104b-1(c)(2)(ii)(B).

[26] Field Assistance Bulletin 2006-03.

[27] A secure continuous access website is a continuously available website that uses authentication and encryption to protect interactions and transactions conducted through the Internet.

[28] 67 Fed. Reg. 17,267-68.

[29] The terms "industry representatives" and "participant advocates" used in this report refer only to those industry representatives and participant advocates we interviewed or who submitted written comments in response to Labor's 2011 request for information. Because this is a nongeneralizable sample, the views presented here do not represent the views of all industry representatives or participant advocates.

[30] 67 Fed. Reg. 17,270.

[31] Some plan sponsors transfer such cost savings to participants, while others do not. In a recent study, we surveyed more than 1,000 401(k) plan sponsors and found that larger plans were more likely to pass recordkeeping fees along to participants than were smaller plans, but that larger plans' typically paid lower fees than small plans. See GAO, 401(K) Plans: Increased Educational Outreach and Broader Oversight May Help Reduce Plan Fees, GAO-12-325 (Washington, D.C.: Apr. 24, 2012).

[32] One service provider reported that Microsoft Outlook includes a delivery receipt function in its e-mail application, but that many other e-mail platforms (e.g., Apple) do not include a delivery receipt function. In addition, this service provider found that often employer e-mail addresses for participants are more prone to non-delivery than personal e-mail addresses.

[33] Labor regulations provide several examples of appropriate measures that are reasonably calculated to ensure that the system results in actual receipt of transmitted information, such as using return-receipt or notice of undelivered electronic mail features, or conducting periodic reviews or surveys. 29 C.F.R. § 2520.104b-1(c)(1)(i)(A).

[34] Another service provider reported that in 2012, 18 percent of their DC plan participants who had the ability to opt-in to electronic delivery did so and 3 percent of those participants already receiving disclosures electronically opted for paper delivery.

[35] Industry representatives also reported that for participants who do not meet the integral part of duties safe harbor, participant inertia may contribute to plan sponsors' difficulty with obtaining affirmative consent for electronic disclosure. However, without confirmation from the participants as to why they did not respond, there is no way to determine whether a participant's inaction resulted from a conscious choice or was the result of participant inertia.

[36] Field Assistance Bulletin 2006-03.

[37] Electronic delivery may have greater implications for participants who are automatically enrolled in a plan. As we have reported in the past, these participants may tend to engage less with their plans. See GAO, Retirement Savings: Automatic Enrollment Shows Promise for Some Workers, but Proposals to Broaden Retirement Savings for Other Workers Could Face Challenges, GAO-10-31 (Washington, D.C.: Oct. 23, 2009).

[38] Several service providers told us that they gather participants' personal e-mail addresses when they access the plan website for the first time and voluntarily provide their e-mail address as a condition of affirmatively consenting electronic delivery. In addition, they said they relied on plan sponsors to send work e-mail addresses of participants who qualified under Labor's integral part of duties safe harbor. One service provider told us that all active employees and participants were asked to provide both work and personal e-mail addresses.

[39] AARP, Paper by Choice: People of all Ages Prefer to Receive Retirement Information on Paper, (Washington D.C.: November 2012). According to AARP, the survey was conducted via telephone omnibus by an independent research company from October 10- October 21, 2012, among a sample of 1,028 respondents ages 25 and older who are currently participating or have ever participated in a retirement savings plan, such as a 401(k) or pension plan. The reported margin of error for total respondents was +/- 3.06 percent at the 95-percent confidence interval.

[40] Currently, a participant's ability to choose electronic delivery is not universal. According to one industry representative, many smaller employers—defined as for-profit companies that employ 100 or fewer employees—do not offer electronic delivery because they do not have an e-mail system for delivery of personnel information and the establishment of an electronic infrastructure is prohibitively expensive. Industry representatives also believed that some small plan sponsors may shy away from offering electronic delivery because of the complex rules involved.

[41] See Exec. Order No. 12,866, 58 Fed. Reg. 51,735 (Oct. 4, 1993) and Exec. Order No. 13,563 (reaffirming and supplementing Exec. Order No. 12,866).

[42] 29 C.F.R. § 2520.104b-1(c)(2)(i)(A).

[43] 67 Fed. Reg. 17,265.

[44] 29 C.F.R. § 2520.104b-1(c)(1)(iv) [Labor]; 26 C.F.R. § 1.401(a)-21(c)(3) [Treasury].

[45] Several participant advocacy groups also noted that reducing the barriers to requesting paper disclosures would further strengthen participant safeguards. One group, for example, suggested that plan sponsors be prohibited from requiring participants to follow unduly

burdensome procedures, such as having to write a letter, in order to register their preference for paper disclosures.

[46] Field Assistance Bulletin 2006-03.

[47] Industry representatives told us that plan sponsors often include statements on electronic disclosures reminding participants of their right to change their delivery preference and method for accessing disclosures; however, they are not required to do so, except with respect to the fee disclosure notice. Although Labor requires plan sponsors that do not use the safe harbor under 29 C.F.R. § 2520.104b-1(c) to notify participants annually of their delivery choice for receiving fee disclosures with instructions on how participants can change their preference, the requirement does not apply to any other required ERISA disclosures under Labor's purview. Technical Release 2011-03R.

INDEX

A

B

C

D

E

F

N

O

P

Q

R

S

T

U

V

W